# ARTHUR RANSOME

# Master Storyteller

by Roger Wardale

SWALLOWS·AND·AMAZONS·FOR·EVER!

GREAT N ORTHERN

Great Northern Books
PO Box 213, Ilkley, LS29 9WS
www.greatnorthernbooks.co.uk

ISBN: 978 1 905080 81 6


Design and layout: David Burrill


CIP Data
A catalogue for this book is available from the
British Library

# Contents

R.D.W

"The words and images in Arthur Ransome's books have been etched in my mind since childhood. Growing up in Derbyshire they unlocked a whole new world, which I soon set my heart on discovering."

*Dame Ellen MacArthur*

# FOREWORD – 1

# by A.N. WILSON

A GOOD WRITER can hold you spellbound by a subject which you do not find inherently interesting. I have enjoyed sailing from time to time, but I have to think twice before being able to identify a windlass, a bowsprit or a bobstay, the jib or the staysail. Arthur Ransome's books make free use of these terms, so much so that I occasionally have to re-read a paragraph to see what is going on; but they are utterly gripping.

As a child, I failed to see the point of them. Someone must have put *Swallows and Amazons* into my hands at the wrong moment. There is always the right moment for a book to grab you. When I first tried to read it, I was numbed with literal-mindedness and could not make head nor tail of it. Just as I'd grasped who Uncle Jim or Roger and Titty were, along came another lot of figures. Ransome's habit of never explaining the fact that these figures are all living in a delightful fantasy during their summer holidays simply baffled me.

Then, later in life, I lined up with the blasé sorts of people who think there isn't much going on in the books, that the narrative pace is too slow, that he is too wordy, too whimsical, too inclined to impose his own childishness on real children.

A good biography by Hugh Brogan, read years ago, suggested to me that Ransome was one of those who did indeed impose his own vision of the world on a group of child-friends, and that there had later been a falling out between him and the Collingwood children, the originals of those who first make their appearance in *Swallows and Amazons*.

A few weeks ago, however, I opened *Swallows and Amazons* once again and was entranced from page one. Not only did I like his way of writing about the children, and the projection of the pirate fantasy into the Lakeland landscape. He evokes nature, its power and presence deftly and economically.

If this is true of the Lakeland story, it is even truer of its sequel, *Swallowdale*, when the *Swallow*, being holed having come aground, the friends are obliged to seek their adventures inland. There are passages in this book of which Wordsworth himself would have been proud.

What I should have conceded to the critics, however, was that there were very great longueurs in both books, and that the pleasure of reading Ransome consisted in savouring the world he conjures up, the relations between the children, their jokey references to pirates, their pemmican picnics and so on.

I was therefore completely unprepared for *We Didn't Mean to Go to Sea*, the next one I tried. Having discovered, after a few pages, that it did not contain my favourite character, Nancy Blackett, Captain of the Amazons, I was disinclined to continue; but I found that I was held by the narrative.

It's about the crew of the Swallows but, instead of the Lake District, the Suffolk coast is the setting. They go out for a short sail with a young man, and fog descends. By a series of mishaps described in terrifying detail, they find themselves out at sea without the grown-up, and John, the eldest of the children, has the task of calming the fears of the others and sailing the boat across – as it turns out – the width of the entire North Sea to Holland.

I can honestly say that it is one of the most exciting pieces of prose narrative that I have read since *Treasure Island*. It is quite literally unputdownable. That is a very considerable gift.

The next one I read is *Great Northern?*, about the discovery of the Great Northern Diver on a Hebridean island and the attempt of an unscrupulous collector to kill it and steal its eggs. Reading this, which also has a gripping narrative, made me think how modern Ransome is, and how much he has in common with the Greens of today. When Dick, the ship's naturalist, glimpses the Great Northern, "it was as if he were an astronomer looking for the first time at a new planet".

The words are almost an echo of Keats. In *Swallows and Amazons*, the children name one hill the Peak of Darien after Keats's sonnet. I, having discovered the Arthur Ransome stories at last, feel "like stout Cortez when with eagle eyes / He stared at the Pacific".

*A.N. Wilson*

# FOREWORD – 2

# by Adam Hart-Davis

The *Swallows and Amazons* were first introduced to me some 60 years ago; I think my mum must have read to me to begin with, although it might have been my sister Bridget. I still recall that vivid description of Roger tacking up the field to hear the cryptic telegram from Daddy – BETTER DROWNED THAN DUFFERS IF NOT DUFFERS WON'T DROWN. Surely Daddy could have included a STOP after the first DUFFERS? But then Ransome clearly wanted the reader, or listener, to be slightly mystified, and so sucked into the story. And what a story. I have read them all several times. I still love *Swallows and Amazons*, but my favourites are *Winter Holiday* and *Pigeon Post* – with *We didn't mean to go to sea* a close third.

My dad was a publisher in London in the 1950s, and he and Ransome (as dad called him) became friends. We even visited Ransome on his little yacht the *Lottie Blossom*, somewhere in Southampton Water I think. He signed my autograph book (long since lost) and drew an instant ink sketch of a dinghy under sail. All I remember is a friendly rotund man with a bald head.

From Ransome's children's books I learned a spirit of adventure, and a love of knots, and sailing, and camping, some of which came in useful in later life. Also little touches – I seem to recall a sketch and description of a dipper, as seen by Titty, somewhere in *Pigeon Post* – and when I first saw a dipper two years ago I recognized it at once from that long-remembered book; such was Ransome's attention to tiny details.

Roger Wardale has produced a lovely book too, warm and friendly. It provides insights not only into Ransome's life and relationships with women, friends, and publishers, but also how he came to write these stories. According to my dad, Ransome made detailed notes about every chapter of each book, until he had planned the plot in minute detail; then he would sit down and write whichever chapter he thought would be the easiest, followed by the next easiest, and so on. So he might write chapter 6, followed by chapter 2, and then chapter 13. My dad even edited, and in some places rewrote, Ransome's autobiography, and one way or another, I don't expect we will ever entirely disentangle fact from fiction over the origins of the Swallows and the Amazons – but at least Roger Wardale offers a delightful and well-researched attempt.

*Adam Hart-Davis*

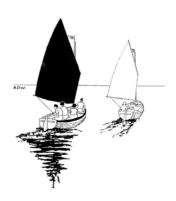

# INTRODUCING ARTHUR RANSOME

THOSE WHO KNEW ARTHUR RANSOME spoke of a large yet child-like man with a drooping walrus moustache, irascible on occasion or deep in gloom, and bursting with enthusiasm at other times, when he would roar with infectious laughter. For all that, he was a shy man who was not particularly comfortable with people unless they shared his enthusiasm for sailing, chess, billiards or fishing.

Looking back on his life, Arthur Ransome once said that he seemed to have lived not one but snatches of half a dozen different lives. An unhappy misfit at school, he became a romantic young bohemian in Edwardian Chelsea, struggling to make his mark as a writer. Escaping from a disastrous marriage to live in Russia, he was caught up in the Great War, turned war correspondent and fell in love with a Bolshevic. During the Russian Revolution he occupied a unique position among foreign journalists, being closer to the Revolutionary leaders than any other westerner, and he was eventually recruited by MI6. He remained in Eastern Europe as the *Manchester Guardian's* Foreign Correspondent until he was able to bring Trotsky's one-time secretary to England as his wife in 1925. They settled in the Lake District and he seemed destined for a successful journalistic career with the *Manchester Guardian*. Finally, in 1929 at the age of 45, and with the prospect of becoming the paper's literary editor, he gambled their financial future on the success of the book that would change his life as well as the direction of children's literature — *Swallows and Amazons*.

The book was no immediate best-seller. The title, as Jonathan Cape recognised, was enigmatic and rather dull. Even less appealing was the absence of pictures, due to its author's instant disapproval of the commissioned illustrations. Fortunately, the book was saved by the good reviews of some of Ransome's friends and Steven Spurrier's splendid map of the lake that Cape used as a cover. *Swallowdale*, its successor that appeared the following Christmas, is effectively the second volume of the same book. Yet after *Swallowdale* Ransome completed ten more novels in the next fifteen years, almost with the regularity of pot-boilers, yet each is completely different from the one before.

*Swallows and Amazons* owes something to *Treasure Island*, a book with which its author expected his readers to be familiar. In writing about Robert Louis Stevenson, his own favourite childhood author, he commented that the secret of his appeal depended 'not on the description of circumstances pleasurable in themselves, but on a tenderness exhibited by the writer for his subject, on the infectious quality of the mood in which a man may look at his past.' In his own case, the misery of his life at prep school only served to heighten the memory of the joys of his early holidays by Coniston Water and The Great Frost of 1895. Nowhere is this more apparent than *Swallows and Amazons, Swallowdale* and *Winter Holiday,* about which he confessed in his *Autobiography* that he had 'a sort of tenderness.'

During the eighty years since the publication of *Swallows and Amazons* in 1930, Arthur Ransome has become almost synonymous with a vision of the innocence of childhood and pastoral England between the First and Second World Wars. To his detractors, the vision is too cosy and middle class; to his devotees it is idyllic. To the young readers of the 1930s it offered a glimpse of the possible and to their successors in the 1940s an escape from the horrors of war and a hope of better things to come.

Arthur Ransome's incomplete *Autobiography* was not published until after his death. Hugh Brogan's fine biography came out in 1984 to mark Arthur Ransome's centenary, the same year as Christina Hardyment's revealing Swallows and Amazons companion *Arthur Ransome and Captain Flint's Trunk*. Since that time a great deal has been written about Arthur Ransome's life and work, much of it published for members of The Arthur Ransome Society. An extensive bibliography by Wayne Hammond was published in the U.S.A. in 2000, and recently two books have concentrated on his life in Russia.

However it is as a master craftsman who excelled in the sublime art of storytelling that this remarkable man is best remembered. The aim of this book is to tell the story of how Arthur Ransome created the twelve Swallows and Amazons novels, of the difficulties that he faced with ill-health and a loving but hypercritical wife, and of the key part played by Jonathan Cape's partner, George Wren Howard.

*Roger Wardale,*
*Bognor Regis, May 2010*

# Chapter One

# THE MAKING OF A WRITER

ARTHUR RANSOME'S DIARY for March 24th 1929 says simply 'Began S&A' but its origin can be found many years earlier when his father carried his eldest son while he was still a baby to the summit of Coniston Old Man, to make amends for Arthur having had the misfortune to be born in a town.

Cyril Ransome was a country-bred academic with political leanings, who had been a scholar and oarsman at Merton College, Oxford. During the term he was Professor of Modern History at the Yorkshire College (now the University of Leeds) and during the vacations, on days when he was unable to go fishing, he supplemented his income by writing history books. In those days Leeds was a pleasant place for a country-lover to set up home, and on most weekends the Professor managed to get in some fishing or shooting. He had been married for two years in 1884 when the first of their four children was born. Arthur Michell was joined by his sisters Cecily and Joyce and brother Geoffrey.

Above all, Ransome's father was passionate about the Lake District, and by passing on a similar emotional commitment to his son, he laid the foundations of *Swallows and Amazons*. Yet their relationship was not an easy one. The Professor never really understood his eldest child and he had some rather bizarre ideas about how the boy should be brought up. On one occasion when his wife Edith was nowhere around, he dropped the naked child over the side of the boat to see if young humans would take to the water as readily as tadpoles. He very soon discovered that they do not.

The death of Ransome's father that occurred when he was 13, prevented the boy from ever securing his complete approval — something that bothered him throughout his life.

His grandfather, Thomas Ransome, was a manufacturing chemist and a farmer on a small scale, and Professor Ransome, having had to clear up one or two debts for him, feared that he could detect similar traits in young Arthur. In the *Autobiography* Ransome describes his grandfather as a first-rate field naturalist and an ingenious fisherman: the ideal companion on country walks, and responsible for laying the foundation of his lifelong interest in natural history. Notes such as 'Redstart at Gilhead' and 'Saw a spotted flycatcher' appear in Ransome's diaries, and when he was housebound in old age he was able to find pleasure at the sight of soaring buzzards from his sickroom window.

His maternal grandfather, Edward Baker Boulton, had been a successful sheepfarmer in Australia when he settled in England from 1860 to 74 and remarried after the death of his first wife shortly after their arrival. He was also a distinguished painter in water-colour — an occupation that he found much more rewarding than sheep farming. Ransome's mother was the eldest of his second family. During one of his periods in England 'EBB' took Arthur to see the Bristol Docks that he had read about in *Treasure Island*. His wife Emma was one of several formidable women in Ransome's life, and from her he learnt the moves in chess — a game that was to give him lifelong pleasure.

Arthur had begun to read at a very early age, and having proved to his father that he had managed to read *Robinson Crusoe* (presumably an abridged version), he was given a copy for his fourth birthday. Reading played an important part of Arthur's childhood, and listening to his mother reading aloud was the highlight of every day. He recalled that his mother read extremely well and that she wisely made a point of never reading books that she did not enjoy herself. Edith had inherited her father's gift for water-colour painting, and years later could be called upon when Ransome was in desperate need of help with the illustrations for the Swallows and Amazons books. Her opinion of each book as it was completed was highly valued and she often undertook to read the proofs. No matter where in the world he was at the time, until her death in

The promenade at Bowness-on-Windremere in Edwardian times with everybody in their Sunday best. (courtesy Ed Goddard)

1944, Ransome tried to send his mother a weekly letter, of which more than 300 have survived.

After a short spell at a day school in Leeds where he was happy and did well, Arthur was packed off to a prep school in Windermere. The Old College was a hearty institution where sporting achievements took precedence over learning and Arthur found himself scorned and bullied. He tried hard to fit in, and in a letter home he begs his mother to go to the animal market and send him some mice so that he could become better friends with the pet-keepers. The letter is full of his hopes for the holidays when he planned to entertain his sisters and brother with conjuring, juggling and his performing animals — mice, rats, guinea pigs and rabbits.

In spite of his pets, he was desperately unhappy during his years at the college and like most small boys in his position he kept his unhappiness to himself. His half-hearted attempt to run away was quickly hushed up by the school authorities that could not, or chose not to recognise it as a cry for help.

In the long summer vacations the whole family took themselves off to the Lake District. Their holiday home was Swainson's Farm in the tiny hamlet of Nibthwaite at the foot of Coniston Water. In eight glowing pages of the *Autobiography* Ransome describes the preparations, the joyful arrival by wagonette from Carnforth Station, the idyllic days spent in 'paradise' and his tearful departure clutching a jar of minnows and boxes of caterpillars.

Of all the pleasures of Nibthwaite the lake held the greatest appeal.

*I had a private rite to perform. Without letting the others know what I was doing, I had to dip my hands in the water, as a greeting to the beloved lake or as proof to myself that I had indeed come home. In later years, even as an old man, I have laughed at myself, resolved not to do it, and every time have done it again.*

So much of those early holidays found its way into the pages of *Swallows and Amazons* and *Swallowdale* — the river, the tarn with its waterlilies, the knickerbockerbreaker, and of course, the lovely little island harbour. There were friendly natives that they met every year — the kindly farmer's daughter, Annie Swainson, who darned his knickerbockers, the charcoal burners, the postman and several gamekeepers. The children joined in the life of the farm, turning the handle of the butter churn and helping with the haymaking, and when they were not needed on the farm, they picked mushrooms or blackberries and tickled trout in the nearby beck.

There were golden days when the family took the Swainson's rowing boat and picnicked on Peel Island. Mrs Ransome was content to take her painting things and sketch while her husband drifted along the shore fishing for trout and, more often than not, would forget to eat his lunch. Meanwhile, the children were free to spend the day much as they chose.

Lake District holidays came to an end with the death of Ransome's father at the age of 46, shortly after Arthur had failed miserably to gain a scholarship to Rugby. He had damaged his foot whilst fishing and what seemed a comparatively minor injury eventually turned tubercular.

THURSTON WATER

W.G. Collingwood's drawing of Coniston Water from the south, for one of the young Arthur Ransome's favourite stories, *Thornstein of the Mere.*

Swainson's Farm in the tiny hamlet of Nibthwaite is only a short distance from the lake. (courtesy Ted Alexander)

The bridge at Nibthwaite where the young Arthur Ransome used to catch fish has been levelled, although the beck still flows underneath the road.

When he was a boy, Arthur Ransome was allowed to steer the *Gondola* with the captain in close attendance. The steamer was launched in 1860 and, after lying derelict for some years, was extensively restored and returned to service in 1980.

A very early photograph of Lanehead, taken around 1860.

The Professor had resigned his chair, as it had already been decided that the family would move to Rugby in anticipation that by living nearer to London he could further his political ambitions and would eventually enter Parliament as a Conservative. He had hoped to be able to keep the family going with some VIth form tutoring and the income from his history textbooks.

Ransome entered Rugby School without a scholarship as a day boy, until a friend of his father found room for him in his House. He described his four years at Rugby School as 'tolerable' and had the great good fortune to come under the influence of a great classical scholar and pioneer of the Direct Method of teaching, Dr W.H.D.Rouse. Rouse discovered Arthur's secret ambition to become a writer, and although what aptitude he showed seemed to indicate a career in science (like his grandfather), he saw enough to encourage this

ambition and did everything he could to help the boy — to the dismay of his mother. Mrs Ransome, mindful of her father-in-law's failed enterprises, was strongly in favour of a safe career in banking or the law.

In 1901 Arthur matriculated and was accepted by the Yorkshire College to read chemistry. He had formed several important friendships at Rugby, notably with Ted Scott, the son of the famous editor, and later owner, of the Manchester Guardian, C.P.Scott.

It was perhaps not the best time for someone who was not wholly committed, to settle to the study of science, for the Arts and Crafts Movement was at its height, reacting against the machine-made 'soulless' goods that were the product of the industrial revolution. He came across J.W. Mackail's *Life of William Morris* and learned of the movement's aim in creating things of beauty as well as function in order to create a more beautiful world. For less than two terms he worked hard reading and writing, but his books had nothing to do with science. He wanted to write fairy stories; he wanted to write essays like Hazlett; he wanted to write for children.

He became a book-collector. Many years later his second wife announced that for every new book he acquired, she was going to insist that he give one away because there was no more room in the house. Not surprisingly, it became clear that he would do badly in his Intermediate Examination, even if he managed to scrape a pass.

Ransome realised that the only way to appease his mother would be to find employment, and the only sort of employment that would satisfy his own ambition would be something in the world of books. He was still only 17 but he managed to persuade his mother to allow him to become an office-boy for the publisher Grant Richards at eight shillings (40p) a week, even though it meant moving to London. It so happened that Mrs Ransome was quite pleased, for publishing was a very respectable occupation, whereas the unpredictable business of trying to scrape a living as a writer was undoubtedly not. She moved house from Rugby to south London and for a time Ransome lived at home.

Running errands for Grant Richards was a foothold, and it enabled Ransome to add penny and twopenny books that were for sale in the Charing Cross Road to his rapidly growing library, but the hours were long and he had not joined the firm to become a publisher. So after six months, he joined the struggling Unicorn Press at more than twice the salary. Once he had been with the firm long enough to be allowed a week's holiday he took the train north to Coniston and found lodgings in the village. It was the summer of 1903. By this time he had already had a few articles and stories accepted by magazines.

There were a number of chance meetings in Ransome's life, but none so fortuitous as the encounter with W.G. Collingwood beside the Coppermines Beck below Coniston Old Man. Collingwood was returning after a painting trip up the mountain when he saw what appeared to be a body stretched out on a rock in mid-stream. Responding to the cry of, 'Are you alive young man?' Ransome explained that he was trying to compose poetry.

Once they introduced themselves they realised that they were not strangers; the families having met whilst picnicking on Peel Island. The result was an invitation to call at the Collingwood home, Lanehead, on the eastern shore of Coniston Water. Lanehead is a fine Victorian property above fields sloping down to the lake shore, facing the village and Coniston Old Man, that some have seen as the origin of Beckfoot. A couple of days later Ransome accepted the invitation and that chance meeting forged friendships that he valued above all others. Collingwood was a true Victorian polymath. He was a fine painter, having trained at the Slade School, an antiquarian, author, President of the Viking Club, and until Ruskin's death in 1900 had been his secretary. His wife Dorrie was an equally talented painter of portrait miniatures. They adopted Ransome and together they gave him the encouragement that he needed in his struggle to become a good writer —support that because of her fear that he would end up like his grandfather, his mother was unable to give.

Emboldened by the Collingwood's ready acceptance that what he was doing was worthwhile, Ransome left the Unicorn Press shortly before it folded, and became a citizen of Bohemia with rooms in Chelsea. He managed to earn enough — or nearly enough — to live, with a mixture of hackwork and ghost writing. The first book to bear his name was *The ABC of Physical Culture* in which he pontificates on such things as 'Smoking', 'Food' and 'Breathing'. He was still managing to read voraciously, claiming for him, that London was marked by bookshops much as buoys marked the sea.

Edwardian London was a good place for an aspiring writer, and for the next six years Ransome was part of a rather raffish set of artists and poets. He drank 'opal hush' (claret and fizzy lemonade) with W. B. Yeats, shared rooms for a while with Edward Thomas and visited Greenwich taverns with John Masefield.

In the summer of 1904 Ransome took himself off to Coniston once more, and for the next few years his life was shaped by summer in the Lake District and winter in London. After a week boarding in the village, he was invited to stay at Lanehead while Robin Collingwood was away at school. The Collingwoods had four children, Dora then aged 18, Barbara 17, Robin 15 and Ursula 13. During his stay, he was under the perceptive eye of Dora who kept a meticulous journal. She noted that 'Mr Ransome' had been to dinner every day since he arrived a week ago and was going to stay with them next day. During the week he had joined the two elder girls spending hours on the water, sometimes until late into the evening, and there had been earnest talk between the three in the lair at the foot of the garden until ten o'clock. A fortnight later he had become 'Arthur'. He remained for seven weeks, and when he left Dora recorded, 'July 24. I have made a bet with him a corncob pipe against a 2d indiarubber that he will come back next year.' For some weeks she had been aware that 'something had been going on' between Barbara and Arthur. After he had left, Barbara confided in her sister. 'She pretends not to care in the least, but I have my doubts!'

The winter of 1904-5 was a particularly congenial time for Ransome. Dora, Barbara and Mrs Collingwood came to Chelsea so that the girls might study art, and stayed in the lodgings that he had found for them. It was inevitable that he should continue to see a lot of the Collingwood sisters. They were introduced to his friends, and he was treated like a member of the family — even after Barbara had turned him down. Very probably she had the good sense to realise they were both too young, for it was another two years before she finally made up her mind to mean, 'No'. For their part the elder Collingwoods found him 'a dear, lovable boy' and would have been happy with the match.

His next two little books are best forgotten, but in 1905 he embarked on a series of three little nature books for children, while he was staying at Wall Nook in Cartmel, where he spent the next three summers. Wisely perhaps, he thought it better not to stay at Lanehead, in spite of the Collingwood's insistence that he would be welcome — though he frequently undertook the long walk to see Barbara, whom he still hoped to marry. *The Child's Book of the Seasons* and *Things in Our Garden* were unremarkable, but in the final chapter of *Pond and Stream* the tone changes and Ransome might almost be describing an afternoon picnic on Peel Island with the Collingwood girls.

*We slip away down the lake rippling the smooth waters, and leaving long wavelets behind us that make the hills and trees dance in their reflections . . .We row down the lake, lazily and slowly, past rocky bays and sharp-nosed promontories, and low points pinnacled with firs. . . A little more than half-way down there is an island that we can see, a green dot in the distance from our farmhouse windows, and here we have our tea.*

Mrs Collingwood's kindly verdict on the books was that they were 'not bad for a little town boy'. He might have continued his apprenticeship with small-scale projects if a friend had not told him that a book of essays about the life in London's Bohemia set against the background of the past was waiting to be written, and he was just the one to write it. He sketched out a synopsis and within two days another friend found him a publisher, and he was off. Although the viewpoint appears to be a distant one, the book has youthful charm in abundance and the evocation of Edwardian London is delightful.

There are portraits of his friends, tactfully referred to as 'a novelist' or by a subtle change of name, and a vivid description of an evening spent with Bohemian friends in an artist's studio, and telling one another of their hopes and dreams, drinking their 'opal hush', singing shanties, listening to stories of 'Annansee the spider' — stories that he would retell himself many times.

The first edition of *Bohemia in London* of 1907 was a substantial book 45 mm thick with 284 pages trimmed with gilt at the top. It was illustrated by fine bold black and white drawings by Fred Taylor, who went on to enjoy a long career as poster artist for the London Underground and London Transport. It was probably the first Ransome book over which the publisher did not lose money and it appeared in American and Canadian editions the same year.

By this time he had developed an interest in the technique of storytelling and successfully proposed to T. C. & E.C. Jack that he edit a series of books to illustrate the range of the subject. On the strength of this assignment he departed for Paris in the autumn of 1907 in order to work on Gautier, Balzac, Merimee and Chateaubriand in the Bibliotheque Nationale.

A career in literary criticism seemed to be opening up for Ransome when he returned to London in the spring of 1908. In the next 18 months nine volumes of 'The World's Storytellers' were published, each with an introduction by Ransome. More importantly, the following year Jack published the combined introductions in *A History of Storytelling Studies in the Development of Narrative*.

Lakeland backwaters in the area visited by Ransome in the early 1900s. The River Crake seen from the bridge at Water Yeat.

All this does seem far removed from *Swallows and Amazons*, but it shows a master studying his craft. He managed to devote a few pages to *Robinson Crusoe*:

*He was in love with verisimilitude and delighted in facts for their own sakes. 'To read Defoe,' wrote Charles Lamb, 'is like hearing evidence in a court of Justice.' No compliment could have pleased him better.*

Among the first reviews of *Swallows and Amazons* appeared the comment, 'One of the great charms of the book is its extreme reasonableness.

Mr Ransome is as thoughtful of detail as Defoe.' Ransome's work echoes that of Defoe in the manner in which episodes taken from life or borrowed from other writers appearing in the Swallows and Amazons books gain appreciably from the metamorphosis. *Robinson Crusoe* was based on Alexander Selkirk's four years of self-imposed exile on a desert island, but as Ransome wrote of Defoe: 'The figure of Selkirk shrinks away like a faint shadow behind that of Crusoe, whose imaginary adventures his own had inspired ...'

Ransome spent the summer of 1908 close to Lanehead and the Collingwoods at Low Yewdale Farm, identified by Christina Hardyment as the model for Dixon's Farm. He had finally accepted that Barbara meant what she said but his romantic feelings for Dora had deepened and their friendship became the talk of the neighbourhood. Fortunately that did not bother Dora, who was very fond of him and echoed her mother's sentiments that he 'really was a dear, in spite of his eccentricities'. Who could resist an exuberant young man who stood in the lane and called up to your window, 'Talking to you is like eating a strawberry ice'?

In fine weather Ransome camped out, and Dora visited his campsite to listen to the tale that he was writing (published with four others that he had written between 1904 and 1910 as *The Hoofmarks of the Faun* in 1910), and on one visit they photographed each other, Ransome tweedy and casual and Dora immaculately turned out and wearing a white boater. At the end of August he proposed. Had he chosen a different occasion, both their lives might have been very different, but Dora was busily engaged on painting his portrait in the loft and did not take him seriously: 'I don't think he really was serious. He seems to want to marry anyone and everyone — anything for a wife!' The following day she noted that Ransome was 'very melancholy' and was packing up to return south.

When they were both housebound at the end of their lives, there was an affectionate and moving exchange of short letters signed 'Beetle' because Dora wore spectacles like the character in *Stalky & Co* and 'Toad' from *The Wind in the Willows* — just as they had when they were young almost sixty years before.

Once back in London, Ransome did indeed behave as if he would do anything to get married, and most of the objects of his affection had enough good sense to see what lay behind the proposal. Then he met Ivy Walker. In the *Autobiography* Ransome claims that his proposal was jocular and that before he realised what was going on, he found himself unofficially engaged. At the end of January he wrote to Dora to announce that he was 'nearly engaged', which she thought very sudden considering that only a short time previously 'his heart had been in a very different place!' On March 13 he married Ivy Constance Walker in Fulham Church and on April 1 the marriage was blessed in Holy Trinity Church in Kensington after they had returned from Paris. It is more than likely that Ransome had come to regret it by the time he reached the altar.

It is difficult to form a balanced view of Ivy and her family. To Ransome, she was a confirmed fantasist who turned ordinary events into melodrama and they certainly seemed to have a malicious sense of humour. The poet Edward Thomas, who was a near neighbour for a while and had found them their first home, saw her for the snob that she undoubtedly was, and did not like her. 'She paints herself. She has many rings. But she is pretty and spiritual and clever, but not clever enough to do her own hair.' When she first met Ivy, Dora Collingwood felt shy and found herself wanting to cry, but after having stayed with the Ransomes for a few days, she came to like her and had no doubt of her love for Arthur. Ivy came from a wealthy family and was attractive and sophisticated but what could she have seen in a penniless writer, decent though he was? Hugh Brogan has suggested that Ivy found Ransome's very unworldliness his real charm, and it is tempting to agree with this assessment.

According to Ransome, Ivy's parents were monsters and their home life appalling and full of hatred. Ransome and Mr Walker tolerated one another, but there was mutual loathing between Mrs Walker and Ransome who did all he could to keep out of her way. What Ransome's family felt about the marriage has not been recorded.

Mr and Mrs Ransome settled close to Petersfield in Hampshire, near — but not too near — the Walker family in Bournemouth.

The essayist, now a literary critic wrote a book on Edgar Allan Poe that lost money, and so did the collection of short stories, *The Hoofmarks of the Faun* when it was published. By then Arthur had become a father. Their daughter Tabitha was born in May 1910 and it was a very great misfortune for both of them that he had only three years in which to enjoy his little daughter. Those three years were anything but easy ones but there were some comparatively happy times. When Tabitha was only a few months old, Arthur, Ivy with the baby and their Jamaican nurse did some house-sitting at Lanehead for the Collingwoods, during which time Ivy helped him in compiling two anthologies, *The Book of Friendship* and *The Book of Love*. Even so, he was beginning to develop stomach trouble and suffer from fits of depression. Was he still hankering after the Collingwood girls?

Shortly afterwards they moved to a medieval farmhouse near Hatch in Wiltshire. While they were living there, Ransome was always off somewhere else, visiting friends, going to see his publisher or staying with his mother. Ivy made little attempt to stop him, though she was clearly unhappy with the situation. She was used to plenty of attention and became frustrated when her husband spent hours at the typewriter and was bad-tempered if he was disturbed. While they were there Ransome bred mice and charmed snakes with his penny whistle and brought one home and kept it in a teapot. There were a few happy and companionable days when Ransome bought a donkey and a cart and they took camping things for a touring holiday but over the next year or so the marriage was to deteriorate further with disagreements on both sides.

Still enjoying his critical role, Ransome wrote one book too many. He turned his attention to a study of the works of Oscar Wilde. Robert Ross, Wilde's literary executor was helpful and supportive but when the book was published Lord Alfred Douglas, Wilde's lover, issued a writ for libel, hoping that he would be able to get Robert Ross, with whom he was having a running feud,

into the witness box. The court found in Ransome's favour, but the months of waiting had taken their toll on his health and he vowed never to write anything that might land him in a similar position again and he renounced critical work and returned to his earlier plan of writing fairy stories.

The other significant work that Ransome began at that time was a study of Stevenson that was thought to have been destroyed, only to surface again after Tabitha's death in 1992. There are 372 handwritten pages of a first draft that will need a lot of work, but hopefully it will be published one day.

In April 1913, free at last from the worry of the impending trial and with Ivy refusing to entertain the idea of divorcing him, Ransome sought a way out of the situation in which he found himself. A recent translation of Russian folk tales set him thinking of visiting Russia where Ivy could hardly be expected to follow, and once in Russia he could make a collection of his own.

Just over one month after the trial, Ransome sailed for Copenhagen.

# Chapter Two

# WITH A FOOT IN BOTH CAMPS

AS HE STEPPED ABOARD the steamer at Tilbury it is not clear whether Ransome had a fixed plan in mind, or whether he was simply removing himself from Ivy's temper tantrums and heading in the general direction of Russia. Things with Ivy had become so unbearable that Ransome's solicitor had advised him to get right away from Hatch for a cooling off period. He scribbled a dockside note to his mother telling her that he was heading for Stockholm and was expecting to be away for three weeks. However, instead of returning to England he finally reached St Petersburg where he was met by Anglo-Russian friends and taken to their country estate in nearby Finland. He found a warm welcome in Terioki amid delightful wooded surroundings and there he established a base from which he made occasional forays into Russia.

Now that he had escaped, his first priority was to learn Russian, and since the Gellibrands spoke nothing else when at home, he had every opportunity to do so. In the *Autobiography* Ransome explains how he taught himself Russian by the use of graduated children's primers, progressing from 'The cat ate the rat' to 'The blue cat ate the purple rat', and so on. He managed to translate a collection of Caucasian tales for which he could not find a publisher, and from time to time he worked on a book about Stevenson.

By the end of September Ransome was back in England. Somewhat unwisely, he returned to Hatch a month later, having allowed himself to be persuaded by Ivy who still believed that she could make their marriage work. That winter Ransome was occupied with a version of *Aladdin* in verse that was finally published in 1919 in a lavishly produced and decorated edition, now much sought-after by collectors. He also wrote a strange allegorical tale for Tabitha called *The Blue Treacle The Story of an Escape* in which Tabitha, rather in the manner of Alice Liddell, was the central character. The little book was not published until 1993 when it appeared under the aegis of The Arthur Ransome Society.

Release came in the form of a commission to write a guide to St Petersburg. Arriving in the middle of May 1914, Ransome pounded the streets of the city by day and poured over his typewriter by night until he had completed the guide in a couple of months. A fortnight later Germany declared war on Russia, Europe was plunged into war and Ransome thought it time to return home.

Resisting Earl Haig's call to enlist because of his poor sight, Ransome offered his services as a Russian correspondent, but found that the newspapers had already established their journalists in Russia, and it was with only a vague commission to write a history of Russia that he returned to St Petersburg (now called Petrograd) at the end of the year.

Ransome had spent the last few days before the outbreak of war becoming friendly with the *News Chronicle* Russian Correspondent, Harold Williams, who was well established in the city and seemed to know everyone of importance. Williams acted as mentor to the aspiring journalist who, for want of regular bulletins to prepare, wrote *The Elixir of Life*, in a little over a month. The tale is an 18th century melodrama with echoes of Edgar Allan Poe, one of the storytellers that Ransome had written about five years earlier. He showed the book to Hugh Walpole who was also in Russia at that time, and having read it he told Ransome that he would have no trouble in finding a publisher. Trusting Walpole's judgement, Ransome sent the manuscript to Methuen, who published the book later that year.

With his novel safely on its way to England Ransome applied himself to the book of folk-stories that was published the following year as *Old Peter's Russian Tales*. Realising that the stories would need quite different treatment for an audience of British children, Ransome created old Peter and his grandchildren Maroosia and Vanya and the hut in the forest where he sits of an evening and tells stories to the children. As he said in the introductory note, 'This is a book written in far away Russia, for English children who play in deep lanes with wild roses above them in the high hedges, or by the small singing becks that dance down the grey fells at home.'

Ransome's friend Dmitri Mitrokhin, who became a greatly respected artist and illustrator, delightfully illustrated the book in colour and black and white. *Old Peter's Russian Tales* has been hugely successful — as it deserves to be — and has remained in print long after the earlier translations disappeared into obscurity.

As Ransome worked away at *Old Peter's Russian Tales* his piles and stomach ulcers became steadily worse, and by July he could no longer endure the pain. He was successfully operated on in Petrograd and convalesced with the Williams family. Just as he was considering returning to England to complete his recovery, Williams brought him the news that the radical *Daily News'* correspondent was seriously ill and Ransome, weak though he was, managed to deputise. His telegrams were welcomed by the editor who asked him to continue the good work, and in this way Ransome's career as a journalist began.

Life became a round of chasing across the city attending press conferences, visiting officials and sending telegrams. At this time there was growing concern among the British community in Russia over the lack of accurate information about the fighting on the Western Front, and Ransome was instrumental in founding an unofficial news agency, The Anglo-Russian Bureau. Ransome was a frequent visitor and Bruce Lockhart, the flamboyant British Consul recalled him as 'a Don Quixote with a walrus moustache, a sentimentalist who could always be counted on to champion the underdog ...' and 'an incorrigible romanticist who could spin a fairy-tale out of nothing'.

It was not until March 1916 that Ransome was given permission to visit the Russian front. He spent a month at the South-Western Army headquarters and returned full of admiration for the Russian soldiers who were successfully holding the front against a much better equipped enemy.

In November Ransome returned to England where he had hoped to be able to secure a position as Professor of Russian Studies in Leeds. He spent a couple of days with Ivy and then for a few days he was able to return to his old life with the Collingwoods. He went rowing on Coniston, walking in the Langdales and visited his mother.

On returning to Petrograd he began to make regular visits to the Russian Parliament (the Duma) in order to increase his understanding of the rapidly changing political scene, although as he told his mother, he feared that if he became too much of a political observer he would have 'no power whatever of playing with imps and other merry devilments through the jolly forests of fairy books'.

On his return to Petrograd he happened to meet a young Polish-American Lola Kinel who was joining her parents in Petrograd, through their mutual love of chess. In her autobiography *Under Five Eagles* she recalled the first Revolution in March 1917 which she witnessed with Ransome, 'It was Grand. All one had to do to feel tremendously exhilarated was to go out into the streets.' Ransome too was caught up in the heady atmosphere: 'There's a gorgeous demonstration going on all over the town today... and red flags and happy people as far as I can see'.

Lola Kinel found Ransome amusing, 'clever yet childish, very sincere and kind and romantic, and on the whole far more interesting than his books'. She remembered his contempt for those who were conventionally or smartly dressed, and saw him as a true Bohemian with a preference for natural Russian girls who did not pose!

In the aftermath of the first uprising, it seemed to Ransome that sooner or later the Bolshevics would form the Government, and since he reported things as he saw them, the Foreign Office were most unhappy with his reports as they did not accord with their preferred outcome. England was many miles away and Ransome went on telling of things as he saw them — and history proved him right.

When at last the October Revolution occurred, it took a great many by surprise — including Ransome, who had slipped back to England for his annual visit. Before he could return to Petrograd there was a great deal of red tape for him to unravel and it was not until Christmas Day that he arrived to find the country on the brink of civil war and the city policed by armed patrols at street corners. By this time Ransome had established a number of useful connections, and a day or so after his return he was interviewing Trotsky, the organising genius among the Bolshevic leaders.

Ransome said that he first met the big girl who had been taking notes during his interview with Trotsky that same evening when she fed him a plate of almost-burned potatoes. Evgenia Petrovna Shelepina was Trotsky's personal secretary and at that time a member of the Bolshevic party. Ransome described her in a letter to Tabitha as a 'fierce revolutionary'. They developed the habit of walking together after work to catch a tram back to the city centre. Slowly but surely they fell in love.

At that time he was seeing Trotsky and Lenin almost on a daily basis and such was his relationship with the Bolshevic leaders that at the time of the Russian New Year (January 14th) he celebrated with the Trotsky children and Karl Radek the Bolshevic's chief of propaganda, whom he considered the most human and cultured of the leaders of the Revolution.

With a Bolshevic (or former Bolshevic) as his mistress and a growing reputation for having sources not available to other Western journalists, it is hardly surprising that there were misgivings in Britain about Ransome's loyalties — misgivings which deepened when Ransome took his stand against intervention by the West.

There is the suggestion in both Lola Kinel and Bruce Lockhart's accounts that Ransome had a romantic view of the Revolution. For his part, Ransome declared that he believed that the Bolshevics were the only party capable of preventing the country from descending into anarchy, and that his role was no more than a go-between working towards the betterment of Russo-British relations. More difficult to swallow was Ransome's refusal to recognise the many atrocities carried out by the Bolshevics although it has been suggested that he knew nothing of these things at the time.

In 1995 the Cambridge historian Professor Christopher Andrew revealed in an article in *The Times* that Ransome had been identified in KGB documents as 'the most important secret source of intelligence on British foreign policy'. There can be no question that both the Soviets and British used Ransome to serve their own ends; the Bolshevics because in addition to the information that he could provide, he would present them in a better light than any other Western observer, and the British because he knew the revolutionary leaders better than anyone else.

Ransome remained in Russia until just before the British took Archangel in August 1918 in support of the White (anti-Bolshevic) Army. Almost all Ransome's British friends had departed, and those remaining were now at risk. Two days

before the internment order came into force Ransome left Moscow for Stockholm by masquerading as a Soviet courier with a Russian diplomatic passport to join Evgenia who had wisely quit her prestigious post in favour of something less conspicuous in the Russian Legation in Stockholm.

Secret Intelligence Service papers released by the British National Archive in 2005 showed that it was whilst he was in Stockholm that he was recruited as agent S76 working under the cover of his reporting activities for the Daily News, although Foreign Office records had revealed the fact some years earlier. At that time there remained many in the West who still saw him as a highly dangerous pro-Russian and some of his personal letters were intercepted by MI5.

At the end of 1918 Sweden broke off diplomatic relations with Russia, partly under pressure from the U.K. Government, and Ransome and Evgenia were expelled. Back in Moscow, Evgenia went to live with her mother, and Ransome after a brief stay, headed for England. Arriving at Kings Cross Station he was escorted to Scotland Yard. On being grilled by Sir Basil Thomson, Head of the Secret Intelligence Service about his politics, Ransome was able to satisfy him that he would not stir up trouble in England by claiming that he only wanted to write his history of the Revolution — and do a little fishing. He never completed his history of the Revolution, but *Six Weeks in Russia in 1919* was hurriedly composed at his mother's house in Kent and immediately published as a simple factual report. It had far-reaching consequences for Ransome. C.P. Snow the editor and owner of the *Manchester Guardian* offered him the post of special correspondent in Russia, the *Daily News* having dispensed with his services when they learnt that he was in the pay of the SIS.

In spite of Foreign Office oppostion, Thomson arranged for Ransome to be able to return to Russia, and if necessary bring Evgenia to England. He travelled via Reval in Estonia, a country at war with Russia, but seeking peace. Ransome was charged with delivery of a message to the Kremlin seeking a settlement. However, returning to Moscow meant a hazardous crossing of no-man's-land between the opposing forces, but Ransome managed to bluff his way through and arranged a meeting with Lenin. He secured the Bolshevic reply setting out their terms for peace while Evgenia packed her bags.

Their return journey to Reval — a distance of around 900 kilometres — was as hair-raising as the outward one had been, for in Evgenia's bags were 35 diamonds and three strings of pearls that she handed to Soviet agents on arrival in Reval. It is hardly surprising that Ransome collapsed with 'brain-fever' as soon as they were safely delivered! The enthusiastic observer of the Revolution in March 1917 had become much too deeply involved by November 1919 — and all because he had fallen in love. A year earlier he had told his mother, ' the Russian Revolution has failed utterly in altering me personally and once I get a little peace and quiet and get my sketch of the development of the revolution written, I shall write FINIS and fetch politics a good boost with a boot in the latter parts, and return with no regrets whatever to pen, ink, tobacco, fishing and the lake country'.

For somebody in Ransome's position such a return to England would hardly have been possible until he had obtained a divorce from Ivy. Once he had recovered, they took lodgings 40 miles west of Reval at the head of Lahepe Bay and for the next four years they lived as man and wife in Eastern Europe until he was free to marry.

Living in Estonia and later in Latvia, Ransome could visit Russia and send the *Manchester Guardian* despatches on the siuation in Eastern Europe free from Russian censorship. He returned to Russia in the spring of 1920 to find that the Cheka (forerunner of the KGB) had raided his Petrograd flat and removed his great collection of newspapers destined for the British Museum and practically everything else except his favourite fishing rod.

As soon as summer came, they acquired an old beach boat that they

Carl Sehmel, the original Peter Duck, who sailed with Arthur Ransome aboard *Racundra* in the Baltic.

christened *Slug* and with the foolhardiness of innocents they sailed 60 kilometres along a strange coast to reach Lahepe Bay, arrived in the middle of the night and fell asleep in the boat. This was Evgenia's first taste of sailing and the experience did nothing to diminish her enthusiasm for more. Nor did the occasions when they planned to go for a sail and found that *Slug* had sunk at her mooring.

The following summer they bought a small cabin yacht, the *Kittiwake*, and although she was too small for satisfactory cruising they took her to sea with a small tender made by local coffin makers and explored the coast, until the *Manchester Guardian* sent Ransome to Riga in Latvia.

The newspaper continued to send Ransome on occasional trips into Russia until 1928, and from time to time until his divorce in 1925 he visited England. Sailing and navigation had taken the place of politics in his scheme of things and the winter of 1922-3 saw the construction in Riga of the famous *Racundra*. Otto Eggers, who was a notable Estonian designer of racing yachts, did his best with Ransome's specification and the result was a nine metre ketch with great beam and shallow draft. No sooner had Ransome took command then he told his mother 'She is very easy to manage…but SLOW.'

The yacht was promised for May 1st, launched at the end of July and finally snatched, unfinished, from the builders yard on August 5th. *Racundra* was taken to the Yacht Club beside the Stint See lake where she was completed by Ransome and the old seaman who looked after the dinghies. On August 20th they set sail with Evgenia relishing her position as Cook and the old seaman that Ransome called 'The Ancient Mariner', happy that he was about to make one more voyage before it was too late.

It was far too late in the year to consider a voyage to England, so they headed north for 60 miles until they landed on the sparsely inhabited island of Runo.

*Our landing on Runo was like a page from Robinson Crusoe or a child's dream of desert islands. . .man, should he appear might be of any kind. Almost, we looked up at the tree tops for pygmies with their poisoned arrows, and watched the trunks of trees for the feathers of one of Fenimore Cooper's Indian braves.*

Ransome's ability to colour events with imaginative romance, that was to be the hallmark of *Swallows and Amazons* and *Swallowdale* shines out from the description.

After negotiating the narrow strait through the Moon Sound from the Gulf of Riga into the Gulf of Finland with a faulty compass, they ran into a storm and had to tack towards Baltic Port under staysail and mizzen alone. When it was light The Ancient managed to repair the damage to the gaff, but instead of going into Baltic Port, Ransome decided to push on for Reval where they made their landfall after a rough, but strangely satisfying passage. The little ship and her crew had not been found wanting. The hours of study that Ransome had spent with the books on navigation, that his mother had sent had proved their worth. So stirred had Ransome been as *Racundra* butted into huge waves that he burst into song.

Things may have become turbulent in the cabin, but Evgenia retained her sense of humour and came on deck with a thermos of soup and the offer of a second to follow if they were going to be drowned before morning.

*Racundra* was in Reval for five days while Otto Eggars conducted a thorough examination and completed the fitting out. Evgenia remained in Reval and a friend on his way to attend a ball in Helsingfors took passage aboard *Racundra*. In Helsingfors harbour a compass adjuster 'swung the ship' and drew up a set of deviations so that navigation would no longer involve a certain amount of guesswork. The return to Reval was a long-drawn out beat to windward in which Ransome and The Ancient took turns to steer. They anchored off the Yacht Club tired out, celebrated with hot rum and water and slept.

It was already very late in the season and they left Reval within 24 hours for the homeward voyage. When the wind died completely Evgenia demanded that they start the engine, but Ransome was no hand with engines and they discovered that The Ancient was no better, whereupon Evgenia told them to throw it overboard, but they told her it was valuable ballast. The rest of the voyage was, to say the least, eventful, though their spirits remained high throughout, until *Racundra* was finally laid up in the safe keeping of The Ancient.

Ransome made two visits to Moscow within four months and while he was away the family home burnt down. Fortunately Evgenia managed to escape unharmed thanks to being woken by her cat, Tom. In December Ransome returned to England and had a meeting with Ivy and their lawyers to discuss arrangements for their divorce. While he was in England he showed his log of *Racundra's* cruise to W.G. Collingwood who declared it a ready-made book and urged him to publish. By Christmas Ransome was well advanced with the book.

On his second visit to Moscow in May 1923 Ransome found himself caught up in another crisis of Anglo-Russian relations. The Foreign Minister, Lord Curzen had sent a list of complaints about Russian offences against British interests, and threatening to cancel British trade agreements and withdraw the British Diplomatic Mission unless the British terms were complied with. The Head of the Diplomatic Mission, R.M. Hodgson had been forbidden to enter into any discussion with the Soviets and when Ransome arrived, it seemed that a fighting reply would be inevitable, leading at best to a fracture of Anglo-Russian affairs. After hours spent in the Kremlin, he managed to arrange an 'accidental' meeting between Hodgson and Maxim Litvinov, the Bolshevic 'roaming ambassador' that resulted in a conciliatory reply. Back in London, Lord Curzen preened himself and announced, 'I think I have gained a considerable victory over the Soviet Government...'

The Ancient had *Racundra* ready for the summer, but it was quite late in the season before they were able to retrace their voyage to Reval. Leaving Evgenia and The Ancient with the ship, Ransome hurried back to England for more talks with Ivy and the solicitors. Nothing had been finally agreed when he returned, and they set sail for Helsingfors once more. They spent a week or so fishing and cruising among the Finnish islands before

Evgenia at about the time of her marriage. (courtesy Brotherton Collection)

returning to Reval where *Racundra* was laid up for the winter.

The economy and clarity that marked his mature writing makes its first appearance in *Racundra's First Cruise* and it was effectively, as Hugh Brogan has observed, 'the first Arthur Ransome book'. It had all been so easy. Less than a week after the return to Riga he told his mother that he had more than 30,000 words and 80 photographs and that when it was revised, he would have 'a very jolly little book', although he regretted there was no feminine interest to speak of.

*Racundra's First Cruise* was published in July with a number of Ransome's photographs. It caused quite a stir in sailing circles and the first print run of 1500 copies sold quickly and the book was published in America later in the year. There is much more to *Racundra's First Cruise* than the description of some sailing in a rather unusual boat. They had made a point of visiting remote islands and isolated communities that were, as yet, untouched by the upheavals of the twentieth century and were described with warmth and sympathy. Perhaps Ransome unconsciously envied their uncomplicated lives.

In the spring of 1924 Ransome returned to England to complete the divorce proceedings. By the terms of what he called a 'frantically bad' settlement, Ransome had allowed Ivy to keep his considerable library as well as one third of his future income. The loss of his library cost Ransome dearly and was something that rankled for the rest of his life, not so much because he needed the books (he knew that he had done his best work in *Old Peter's Russian Tales* and *Racundra's First Cruise* without any books at all), but because they had become a part of him and the matter had become a matter of principle.

On May 8th 1924 the 'Master and Owner of *Racundra'* married 'The Cook' at the British Consulate in Reval. Those who remembered Evgenia spoke to me of her large size, her strength, her deep voice and mildly amusing accent that was not always easy to understand but very easy to imitate. Friends were greeted with a warm hug, and some delicacy that she had just made or bought would be thrust upon them. She was hasty-tempered, quick to judge, argumentative and given to exaggeration. She joined her husband in fishing, sailed with him, nursed him, shared his love of nature, was a corrective to his more airy-fairy moods and intensely loyal throughout their 40 years of marriage.

To the end of her days Evgenia claimed that she was being watched by the K.G.B. Was this no more than far-fetched imagination? Those who knew her in later life understood that the subject of Russia was taboo, and after she visited her family as a British citizen shortly after her marriage, Evgenia did not return to see them again until 1972.

By way of a honeymoon they set out from Riga in August and took *Racundra* for a leisurely fishing cruise up the long and winding Aa River and at the beginning of November they were in England.

# Chapter Three

# SWALLOWS AND AMAZONS

EDITH RANSOME WROTE to welcome Evgenia into the family and ended her letter with the words, 'I do hope that when we meet we shall understand one another and become very good friends.' Their friendship was cemented within a few weeks of Evgenia's arrival in England, for she had to spend the two months over Christmas with her in-laws, Ransome, having been packed off to Egypt by the *Manchester Guardian*, to cover the assassination of the British Governor-General.

By middle of February 1925 Ransome was home, and they were able to begin house hunting. In allowing him to return to England, the *Manchester Guardian* had stipulated that he must live within easy reach of Manchester, and to Ransome this meant an opportunity to settle in the Lake District.

Within three weeks they had found and bought their dream home. Low Ludderburn is a whitewashed stone cottage around four hundred years old situated some six miles south of the town of Windermere, standing beside a sharp bend in a narrow country road. The cottage stands about 400 feet above sea level, well sheltered by yew trees in the garden and the higher ground to the north but commanding a broad view to the south across the valley of the River Winster and to the east for 40 miles into Yorkshire. The building is a typical vernacular farmhouse, two up, two down with impressively thick walls, a slate roof, low ceilings and a sturdy stone lean-to. It is so isolated that it merits an inclusion in the Ordnance Survey touring map of the Lake District. Beside the road and at right angles to the cottage stands a large

barn approached by some hazardous slate steps where both Ransomes had accidents. Evgenia saw the barn's possibilities at once, and by the addition of two large windows, a very fine wooden floor and a fireplace, the upper floor was converted into Ransome's finest workroom. The first five Swallows and Amazons books were completed here, with Ransome pacing up and down the room at difficult moments.

The cottage was without gas, electricity or telephone, and their water had to be carried from a spring on the fell nearby. Ransome mentions cooking on a 'Perfection' stove. This was a popular make of oil-burning stove with three burners — just about sufficient for Evgenia, who was an elaborate cook. Life at Low Ludderburn without a car would have been impossible, and Ransome acquired what he called 'a perambulating biscuit tin ... that rattles about beautifully' and soon collected a number of dents. In due course a wooden garage was built to house the car, and is still standing today. In fact the cottage and the surrounding area has changed surprisingly little since the Ransomes were living there and the snowdrops that Evgenia planted on the roadside verge still make a grand display in early spring.

Almost their only neighbours were Colonel Kelsall who had recently retired from the Royal

**Low Ludderburn at the time it was the Ransomes' home. (From a photograph)**

Looking over Low Ludderburn rooftops across the Winster Valley towards Barkbooth and the distant Yorkshire hills.

The one-time barn at Low Ludderburn became Arthur Ransome's finest workroom, and the wooden garage that was built to house 'rattletrap' still stands beside it.

The snowdrops that Evgenia planted on the roadside verge by Low Ludderburn still flourish each year.

Jonathan Cape's dignified premises in Bedford Square. In old age Arthur Ransome fell from the front steps – an accident from which he never fully recovered.

Engineers and his family who lived at Barkbooth, a mile or so away across the valley. The Colonel and his two small sons, Desmond and Richard (or Dick), shared Ransome's enthusiasm for fishing, and the men frequently fished together in the rivers on Windermere. In the early years at Low Ludderburn, Ransome kept a rowing boat at Storrs, south of Bowness, for the express purpose of lake fishing. Fortunately their wives found a common interest in solving crossword puzzles.

Another military man, Colonel Hudson, who lived in Bowness, had two young daughters, Joan and Peggy, and sometimes the four children were invited to the barn for parties that Evgenia had a habit of turning into feasts. Ransome played his accordian and led the sea shanties with great shouts. Once Ransome commenced to write the Swallows and Amazons books, the four children provided Ransome with a perfect sounding board on which to try his latest chapter.

A chance remark to Ted Scott, soon to become the editor of the *Manchester Guardian,* one day had profound career consequences for Ransome. The two men had been at Rugby together, and Scott knew full well that Ransome had had his fill of political journalism. So when Ransome complained that the paper was not doing enough for fishermen, Scott offered him a weekly column to do more or less what he liked with. The result was the famous 'Rod and Line' column that ran most weeks (except when he was sent abroad) from mid-August 1925 to mid-September 1929. The column was written with the enthusiasm, simplicity and illuminating clarity that had marked *Racundra's First Cruise*, and its humorous slightly self-depreciating tone brought him a loyal readership that included many who had never wielded a rod.

Meeting the house purchase price of £550 entailed the sale of *Racundra*, something they contemplated with great regret, but it would scarcely have been practical to keep the yacht in England so long as they were living in the Lake District.

From time to time a telegram would arrive at Low Ludderburn and Evgenia would be left alone while her husband was off somewhere or other. Evgenia had to spend her second Christmas in England without Ransome, when C.P.Scott wanted him to discover to what extent Russian influences were at work in China. Ransome still had the ability to sum up a political situation quickly and

report clearly to his paper but he was now leaving his much-loved 'missis' and his heart was not in it, as he told his mother. 'I am all for slippers and a pipe, a glass of hot rum and the quiet life.' He was 43 and his ulcer was beginning to trouble him again.

One day Ransome met Jonathan Cape at a party given by a mutual friend, the writer and future MP, Molly Hamilton, who had tried earlier unsuccessfully to persuade Cape to publish *Blue Treacle*. Instead, Jonathan Cape gave Ransome the chance to return to the sort of work that he had been doing 20 years earlier in order to build up a collection of books bearing his name that would support him in his old age. He still thought of Ransome as an essayist and wrote to say that he thought that there was room for another book to be written which dealt with people on the borderline when genius goes hand in hand with excess and if Ransome cared to write it he would guarantee to publish it.

Ransome was not tempted although it set him thinking that the best of his 'Rod and Line' articles would make a cheerful little book. In early 1927, Jonathan Cape approached Ransome again with a view to republishing *Racundra's First Cruise* in their Travellers' Library — a series of reprinted books that Cape thought were likely to be in permanent demand. The volumes were pocket-sized and well-produced and the series proved extremely popular. Ransome readily agreed, as did the original publisher, Unwin. In this way the long and highly successful association between Ransome and the House of Cape had its beginning.

Jonathan Cape was a few years older than Ransome, and like him he began his career as a book-trade errand boy in London, before he moved on into publishing. In 1921 he formed the company that bears his name, in partnership with George Wren Howard. Cape was largely self-educated, and had worked his way up from the bottom, but Howard was a product of Marlborough and Cambridge. Together, they became arguably the outstanding publishers of quality books of their generation.

The company had become established in 30 Bedford Square, round the corner from the British Museum. Cape wrote, 'the finely proportioned rooms, wide entrance, air of dignity, and solid worth, can have only have a good influence on those who work therein.' The whole enterprise was housed on three floors of the building. The stock

Titty, Susie, Roger, a friend and Taqui at Coniston in 1928. (From a photograph)

Taqui Altounyan, Brigit Sanders and Roger Altounyan with a model of *Mavis* in Brigit's garden at Nibthwaite.

Bowness Bay, Windermere, 130 years ago. It is interesting to compare this photograph with the same scene today.

Bowness-on-Windermere is at its best when seen from across the bay. Arthur Ransome's earliest sketch map of the lake showed the island, Darien and Holly Howe but there is no suggestion of Rio Bay.

There is a brief glimpse of the lake as you go down the last steep drop into the village that the Swallows and Amazons called Rio.

There are several possible Dariens around Coniston Water and Windermere. Perhaps the most convincing is Gale Naze Crag at the head of Windermere between the River Brathay and a deep bay.

was kept in the basement where the books were packed and invoiced for dispatch. On the ground floor the secretaries worked in a large office beside the front door, while at the rear of the building was the Trade Counter. Books were hoisted up from the packing room for London booksellers to collect at the back door. Upstairs were the imposing offices occupied by the partners, while the advertising department had to make do with the half-landing. By the time that Jonathan Cape became my publisher more than 50 years later, they had moved to similar premises next door and the place had an air of slightly faded gentility.

Ransome's final visit to Russia took place in February 1928 when he was called upon to make sense of the rapidly developing situation in Moscow, following the rise of Stalin. He saw Litvinov but Karl Radek and Trotsky were in exile. Evgenia was left with the car out of action and no food or money in the house and she had to walk to Windermere. Fortunately it was a lovely day so that she enjoyed the exercise.

Back in England Ransome wrote a series of nine major articles, 'An Enquiry in Russia', and on April 21 he met Dora Collingwood and her family off the train at Windermere.

Dora had met her husband, Ernest Altounyan, through his friendship with her brother Robin. He too was a Rugby man, although not contemporary with Ransome, being five years his junior. Like Ransome before him, Altounyan was welcomed into the Collingwood family home and the two had married in 1915, at the time that Altounyan was working in the Middlesex Hospital. Four years later they moved to Syria so that Altounyan could assist his father in running their celebrated hospital in Aleppo.

Ernest Altounyan was of Armenian-Irish descent and throughout his life claimed that he was more of a poet than a surgeon. Also like Ransome, he had learnt to sail with the Collingwoods on Coniston Water, and a fortnight after the families' arrival at Coniston he went to Barrow in Furness and bought two dinghies that they renamed *Swallow* and *Mavis*, so that his children could begin to learn to sail. These were Harriet known as Taqui who was almost eleven, Susie aged nine, Mavis known as Titty who was nearly eight, Roger aged six and Brigit who was not quite two.

Dora noted in her journal that Ernest returned with one of the boats at one o'clock the following

morning. The story goes that he arranged with Ransome that they would share the cost and at the end of the summer, after their return to Syria, one of the boats would become Ransome's.

The family stayed at Bank Ground Farm, a short distance down the field from Lanehead, as both the Collingwood grandparents were past having noisy youngsters in the house. The story of the young Altounyan's summer of 1928 has been retold and embroidered until it has become largely mythical. There are a number of entries on the internet that purport to tell of the creation of *Swallows and Amazons*, saying something along the lines of 'The Altounyan children spent the summer learning to sail with Arthur Ransome and later he wrote of their adventures in *Swallows and Amazons*'. To this Ransome would have snorted, 'Tosh!' and would, I believe, have been deeply upset.

It is very difficult to prove a negative but I have searched every known source for some documentary entry that would support this assertion — and failed. Neither in Ransome's or Evgenia's diary is there any suggestion that he was engaged in giving sailing lessons or that he sailed with the Altounyan children, though Evgenia refers to sailing with their father in *Beetle*, before he had bought the *Swallow* and *Mavis* dinghies. Dora's journal makes no mention of any sailing lessons during the rather wet summer of 1928, though she does mention Ernest spending all day on the lake with the children as soon as they arrived at Coniston, leaving everyone else to do the unpacking. There is also a mention of the time that they raced in three boats around Peel Island. On another occasion she and Ernest took a boat down to Peel Island and had a terrible, squally time getting back up the lake. If they were sailing the narrow *Mavis*, they would indeed have had a terrible time, for the dinghy became unstable in anything of a blow, and on one occasion capsized with fatal consequences. It would be difficult to imagine a less suitable dinghy for small children to learn to sail. Having said that, *Mavis* became a much-loved boat and was sailed by various members of the family for sixty years.

In her delightful childhood memoir, *In Aleppo Once*, published in 1969, Taqui Altounyan says nothing about any sailing lessons, only that Ransome had stood at the end of the pier by their boathouse and watched them. Years later, shortly before she died, she confided that there had been no more to it than that. As for their adventures together, the Altounyans always stoutly maintained that they never did any of the things in the stories — although they would love to have done. As is usually the case, the myth is so much more attractive than the reality.

For the remainder of 1928, Ransome produced the weekly 'Rod and Line' essays without a break, wrote two leaders and reviewed 43 books. Not since 1913 had he spent so long in England at one time. At the end of the summer the *Swallow* was transported to Windermere as arranged, and on October 20th Ransome was able to introduce Ted Scott to the delights of dinghy sailing. Just before Christmas *Swallow* was put into Borwick's (the boatbuilders in Bowness Bay) shed for the winter. The following day he wrote a doleful letter to his mother, 'I'd have liked to send you a new book by myself. But I haven't written one and I begin to feel I never shall again.' The only creative writing Ransome had managed that year was to write a jolly version of *Aladdin* for Ted Scott's daughter, Peggy and her friends to perform at school.

It was more than ten years since Ransome worked on the Russian folk-tales and he was badly in need of a strong motivational shove. When it came, it was from an unexpected quarter. The Altounyan's visit to England was coming to an end and Ernest had indicated that he was planning to pay them a visit. The relationship between the two men, never cordial, had cooled to such an extent that by December, Ransome was wishing Altounyan would return to Aleppo before there was a violent quarrel. So when he announced that he was coming one afternoon in January Ransome reluctantly agreed, but said that if he came at all he was to leave the children behind, as he was up to his eyes in work. A couple of days later from his workroom he heard children's voices below. Thoroughly put out, he hurried down to find Taqui and Titty each bearing a red Turkish slipper — a belated birthday present. His bad temper evaporated and he was touched by the gift that had been bought for him in an Aleppo souk. Only when he thought that it was safe to do so, did Altounyan appear from behind the wall where he had been hiding. All work was forgotten, and the following day Ransome and Altounyan spent aboard *Mavis* wallowing about in a flat calm while the rest of the family were preparing for their departure. Ransome wrote several accounts of how he came to write *Swallows and Amazons*, some of which

are misleading, as they were probably intended to be, and do not square with diary entries and surviving notes. The two accounts that Ransome wrote for *The Horn Book* (an American literary journal) and *Young Wings* (the magazine of The Junior Literary Guild) to coincide with the publication of *Swallows and Amazons* in America contain much that is poetic licence, but appear to be the most reliable. Both were published in February 1931, six months after publication.

Having told the story of the birthday gift and his wish to do something for the children in return, he goes on, 'Obviously the thing to do was to write them a book about their little *Swallow* they were leaving behind.' The hero of *Swallows and Amazons* was to be the little sailing boat itself, but as Ransome says in *The Horn Book*, 'in writing about children, one is writing about ones own childhood as well as theirs, and so, in a way, about childhood in general'. Both *Swallows and Amazons* and *Swallowdale* were enriched by Ransome's cherished memories of his Nibthwaite holidays thirty years earlier.

Having established that memories of Ransome's childhood played their part in the creation, it is worth remembering that Ransome, like Captain John, was the eldest of a family of two boys and two girls. However, there can be no doubt that Able-seaman Titty and the Ship's Boy Roger owed a little more to the Altounyans than just their names, for Ransome wanted to make Titty and Roger Walker sufficiently like their namesakes that they could believe that the book was about them. Susie was nothing like Susan Walker, as her school friends were relieved to find out when she came to England at the age of 13. For a while Taque was content to believe that she had been turned into a boy and to sign her letters to Ransome, 'Captain John'.

However, to say that the family from Syria were the originals is going too far. The Walker children were quintessentially English, whereas the Altounyans had been brought up in Syria, and when at last they were sent to school in Windermere they had problems with the other girls who unkindly called them 'The Three Zulus', just as their father in his day had been called 'The Turk'. They were considered 'peculiar' at school and were asked to try not to be quite so different. The Altounyans were not the only youngsters that Ransome had come into contact with. As well as his near neighbours Desmond and Dick Kelsall, he

Peel Island (Wild Cat Island) is the object of pilgrimages by enthusiasts from all over the world.

A glimpse of the hidden harbour at the south end of Peel Island.

A closer view of Peel Island harbour. (courtesy Ted Alexander)

In *Swallows and Amazons* the Swallows waited among islands as the sun set and wished that they could hurry it on its way.

also knew a local family of intrepid campers that were to be found every summer beside Coniston Water, spending their days sailing and fishing. The Sumner children were John (aged 11 in 1928), Nancy (9), Margaret, known as Peggy (4). The coincidence is too great to be dismissed lightly, but unfortunately, very little more is known about them.

Ransome claimed that Nancy and Peggy 'had sprung to life one day when, sailing on Coniston, I had seen two girls playing on the lake shore'. Most of his sailing on Coniston had taken place years earlier, but it is quite possible that he was referring to the Sumner girls.

Much has been written about the dearly loved Arcadian landscape of the five Lake District novels. Suffice to say that the lake is broadly Windermere with a little of Coniston Water added, and the country around the lake is a mixture of the two surroundings. Anyone searching for Darien, the Beckfoot Promontory and Horseshoe Cove by drifting around the lakeshores of Windermere should not be disappointed. Wild Cat Island itself is mostly Peel Island of his early picnics, disguised with what W.G. Collingwood called 'literary camouflage'.

But before Ransome could start to write, Evgenia and he had to face a life-changing decision. C.P.Scott, then in his 57th and final year as editor of the *Manchester Guardian,* called Ransome to the office, knowing full well that Ransome did not want to leave England, in order to ask him to go to Berlin at the end of April on a salary of more than £1000 per annum. He had, as he thought, a juicy carrot: after serving a couple of years, Ransome could return to Manchester and become literary editor.

The last thing Ransome wanted was to spend the rest of his working life in the Manchester office and he returned to Low Ludderburn in deep gloom. The crunch came in the middle of March when Scott said that he wanted Ransome to go to Berlin at the earliest possible moment. Ransome had just finished making arrangements to have *Swallow* put in the water, and the timing could hardly have been worse. Fortunately, Evgenia and he had had sufficient time to talk the possibilities through, and with her full support, on March 19th Ransome went to Manchester, prepared to get the row over and to resign with effect from the end of June. After that time they would have to manage on the fee for his weekly essays, the income from

books (if any), book reviews and the occasional leading articles.

In one of his accounts, Ransome mentions that the story of *Swallows and Amazons* came to him whilst sailing in *Swallow*, and this seems to have been so. On March 23rd, they had their first really good sail of the year. The morning began misty with a dead calm, but by mid-afternoon the wind had picked up a little and so they collected *Swallow* from Borwicks at 4 o'clock and decided to try for Storrs, where they hoped to have tea in the hotel. It was a steady beat down against a light southerly wind and they were only just in time to be served. The return sail in the dusk was idyllic and Ransome had plenty of opportunity to allow his mind to wander. He says that same evening he began to put down some thoughts. In Ransome's diary the following day's entry carries the famous note, 'Began S&A'.

All that has survived from the very early planning is a list of names and ages, a sketch map showing a lake with some islands and a list of chapter headings. The crew of the *Swallow,* whose name was Smith (later changed to Walker) is Dick (from Kelsall or Scott) later changed to John aged 12, Susan aged 10, Titty aged nine, Roger aged six and Vic aged one and a half who 'does not count'. The Amazons (whose name is Smith) are Jane aged 13, Mary whose proper name is Ruth, aged 12 and Tom aged three. There was also the Houseboat Man whose name was Turner.  In a later note Roger has aged by a year and Vic has become Victoria whose proper name is Bridget. The Amazons are now Nancy and Peggy and they have a young brother, Tom. The changes seem to have been made when Ransome substituted names from the Sumner family. Why ever he should choose to give his fictional family the name of his first wife has never been explained. John Walker was the name of one of the Bowness boatman and Walker's boatyard on the Ferry Nab cared for *Swallow.*

It is possible to form some idea of the plot by means of Ransome's list of chapter headings. The Swallows' captain has not yet become John and the Amazons are still Jane and Mary, who are 'ruthless'. The chapters telling of the war, with the Swallow's cutting-out expedition and Titty's fortunate capture of the *Amazon,* appear earlier in the proposal and the further outline seems to be more complex and warlike than the final version. There are references to a 'second arrow' and

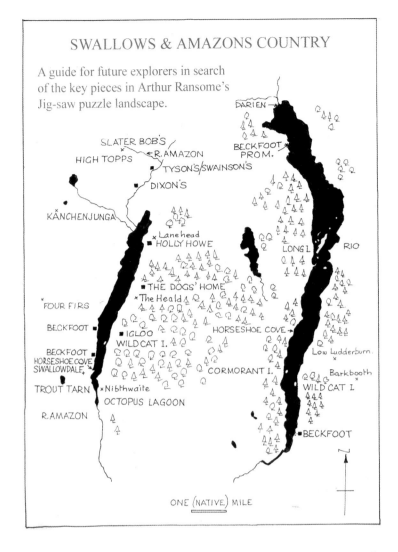

## SWALLOWS & AMAZONS COUNTRY

A guide for future explorers in search
of the key pieces in Arthur Ransome's
Jig-saw puzzle landscape.

DARIEN

SLATER BOB'S
HIGH TOPPS
R. AMAZON
BECKFOOT PROM.
TYSON'S/SWAINSON'S
DIXON'S
KANCHENJUNGA
Lanehead
HOLLY HOWE
LONG L.
RIO
THE DOGS' HOME
The Heald
FOUR FIRS
BECKFOOT
IGLOO
HORSESHOE COVE
WILD CAT I.
Low Ludderburn
BECKFOOT
HORSESHOE COVE
SWALLOWDALE
CORMORANT I.
Barkbooth
WILD CAT I.
TROUT TARN
Nibthwaite
R. AMAZON
OCTOPUS LAGOON
BECKFOOT

ONE (NATIVE) MILE

'prisoners' and 'rescue'. Once the 'treasure' has been discovered, the Swallows and Amazons, in true storybook fashion, set out to catch the burglars and the book concludes with their successful identification through the registration number of their motor car.

Ransome created his working space on a large blanket-covered table. Apart from his typewriter, the table was home to a number of keepsakes that he had picked up on his travels. There was an ancient Russian brass and enamel ink-well, a Russian ash-tray in the shape of a duck, a peasant doll, two or three cat figurines, a lucky stone with a hole from the summit of the Old Man of Coniston, a tiny telescope, a 'bun' penny (early Victorian), a George III penny, a pocket compass and two retractable candlesticks for use when reading on train journeys — also relics from his time in Russia. As well as the keepsakes and a space for books, there was a blotter, a tin of pen-nibs and his pencils, each with a Turk's head knot around its middle to stop it from rolling off the table. Evgenia, not unkindly, referred to his collection as his 'toys'.

From the wall of the barn a large stuffed fish in a glass case looked down at Ransome as he worked and a comfortable reading chair stood alongside the window. In later years Dora Altounyan's portrait of Titty aged about twelve had pride of place.

Carried along on a wave of enthusiasm, Ransome had completed the first 45 pages by the end of the month and managed several good long sails in *Swallow* before going to London to offer 'The Swallows and The Amazons' to Jonathan Cape. He stayed with Molly Hamilton and let her read the precious pages. She liked them immensely and after publication wrote two of the most enthusiastic reviews. Thus encouraged, Ransome prepared for his meeting with Cape who accepted *Rod and Line* as the first of the books of essays and encouraged Ransome to settle down to a series on more general subjects. Diffidently, Ransome told Cape about his new story. Cape glanced at the list of chapters and announced that he would publish it and pay an advance of £100 on publication. 'But it's the essays we want!' he added.

He never got them. More than one million copies of *Swallows and Amazons* were sold in the first 20 years. Even eighty years after publication, the book has been selling at the rate of many thousands of copies a year. It has been translated into numerous languages. It was dramatised for radio in the mid-1930s and adapted and read by Derek McCulloch in Children's Hour in the 1940s. More recently it was featured in the BBC Radio Four series 'On the Trail of the Swallows and Amazons'. A very successful feature film starring Virginia McKenna and Ronald Fraser

Often a fine day on Windermere is heralded by a misty, almost colourless, start. It was just so on the morning of the Swallows' cutting-out expedition to the Amazon stronghold in *Swallows and Amazons*.

The mouth of the River Crake (River Amazon) with its deep reed beds where the Amazons hid on the night of the Swallows' cutting-out expedition. A short distance downstream is Allan Tarn (Octopus Lagoon) and the waterlilies.

Heather Beal and David Cormell recreating Mary Swainson darning Roger at Yew Tree Farm (a possible Swainson's Farm).

The boathouse down the field from Bank Ground Farm (Holly Howe) from which the *Swallow* with Captain John at the helm set sail into uncharted waters.

When making the BBC Radio Four series, 'On the Trail of Swallows and Amazons', the team were based at Bank Ground (Holly Howe). Back – Producer Andy Cartwright, Heather Beal, Lucy Batty of Bank Ground, Jack Young, Friendly Native Claire Kendal-Price. Front – David Cormell, Kimberley Hale, Friendly Native Roger Wardale.

appeared in 1974, following a less successful adaptation for television in 1965. In 1985 it was adapted for the stage and recently there have been proposals to produce a musical version and another adaptation for television.

A few days after his return north, Molly Hamilton went to stay and was duly taken out in *Swallow*. For several days after her return to London, Evgenia and he enjoyed an orgy of sailing in the southern basin of Windermere, and on one occasion they took one of their cats for a sail. Whenever he was not sailing, Ransome swept ahead with his first draft. Having finished a chapter he called 'The Parley', he took stock. He had completed The Peak in Darien, Voyage to the Island, First Night on the Island, Skull and Crossbones, First Arrow, and The Parley. These were followed a couple of days later by Leading Lights and The Charcoal Burners. By the end of April Ransome had added 'A Visit to Captain Flint', 'The Birthday Party' and 'A Fair Wind', giving him more than half of his anticipated 240 pages. With the exception of the final chapter, he wrote the first draft in chronological order — something that was not often the case with later books. The first draft reached 253 pages and was completed in the middle of May — just under two months! No wonder that he remarked years later that 'It almost wrote itself'.

Ransome felt quite childish about his new project and in a revealing passage in his autobiography he tells how he would take the loose-leaf binder with the precious typescript and put it beside his bed in order that he could reach out and touch it if he awoke during the night.

An almost complete draft called 'The Swallows and The Amazons' and dated 1929 is held in the Ransome Collection at Abbot Hall in Kendal. It was published in a limited edition for members of The Arthur Ransome Society in 1997. The draft follows the familiar plot until the morning after the night of high adventure on the lake, when it splits into two versions. In general, the draft contains more technical detail about sailing and cooking and additional dialogue than the published version, in which the plot moves with greater economy and vigour as a result.

The first change anybody coming to the draft will notice is that the Swallows are staying at a farm called Bank Ground rather than Holly Howe. Once they are safely on the island, John slips off while the others are preparing their first meal and he alone discovers and successfully enters the harbour in *Swallow*. The others, knowing nothing of all this, think that someone has taken *Swallow* while they had been busy round the fire preparing their first meal.

Once the Swallows are safely on the island there are two short chapters, 'Cormorants' and 'Settling Down' in which they collect the milk from Dixon's Farm and John and Roger sail to Rio to buy rope for the lighthouse tree and to call in at Bank Ground on the way back to the island for their fishing rods and bathing things. After dinner they all sailed in *Swallow* and see the cormorants fishing from Cormorant Island. The following day is spent fishing and cooking the perch for supper.

The following morning they see the Amazon pirates for the first time. Ransome was always careful to avoid references to the appearance of his Swallows and Amazons and his mention of the Amazons' curly hair in the draft was later removed. The draft follows the familiar course until the chapter 'Taking Breath' where there are two versions. In one there is an extended account of chart-making, while Roger was catching minnows in the harbour. The large mountain is named Popacatapetle and they have heard that there is a river at the head of the lake, and that is marked as 'Reported River'. Titty's islet in Rio Bay is called Spyglass Rock — a much more evocative name — and the lake is decorated with pictures of whales and sea-serpents.

In the second version John visits mother and later that day Titty tells John and Susan that she heard two pirates burying treasure on Cormorant Island. They think she is romancing and Susan, in particular is dismissive — '"Oh look here, Titty," said Susan almost turning native again,' which was changed to a more kindly, '"Steady on, Titty"'.

The following morning, after Titty and Roger collect the milk for breakfast and have reported that Mrs Dixon asked them if they had been at the houseboat, they are allowed to row across to Cormorant Island with a hammer for a pick-axe to look for the treasure, while John keeps an eye on them through the telescope.

While John is doing a little sailmaking and Susan tidies the camp in readiness for the arrival of the Amazons they are interrupted by Sammy the policeman investigating the burglary of the houseboat. The Amazons turn up in the middle of the questioning and send the policeman packing. John lets out that Captain Flint had called him a liar and Nancy hurries off to tip him the black spot.

The next chapter describes how Titty and Roger find the treasure, and having left Roger sitting on the treasure chest on guard, Titty returns to Wild Cat Island to fetch John and Susan. To her horror she finds Captain Flint and the Amazons in camp, but before she has time to hide, Nancy spots her.

Titty finds that Captain Flint is completely friendly, and she learns that the burglars stole his box with the book that he had been writing all summer. Questioning him about the box, she discovers that their treasure chest contains the missing book and she tells him what they have found. They arrive on Cormorant Island where Roger is still guarding the treasure. Captain Flint carves the wooden fish with its sermon to leave in place of the box, before agreeing to join in a war in a day or two.

The next chapters that describe the battle in Houseboat Bay and the storm are much like the book.

In the second version Titty lets Roger into the secret of the buried treasure. Next day Roger and Titty are allowed to go treasure hunting, but it is Roger who comes breathless into camp with the news of their discovery. When the Amazons see the treasure, they shout together, 'It's Uncle Jim's box!'

In a short extract of a possible third version, the only thing that Titty and Roger find is a pipe. 'I'm afraid it will have to be written off as a bad job,' said the Houseboat Man.

There are two versions of the final chapter. In one, the holiday ends with a feast on the houseboat during which Captain Flint gives Titty the parrot and it is clear that neither the battle nor the banquet that followed have taken place, for Nancy tells Captain Flint, 'Properly speaking you should have been made to walk the plank.'

The second version follows the familiar story of the visit of the natives, packing up and the final voyage to Holly Howe via Horseshoe Cove.

Ransome was still undecided about the last third of the book around the time that his notice to the *Manchester Guardian* ran out and the paper gave him a new opportunity to secure a regular income. For a number of years the *Manchester Guardian* had carried a prestigious 'Saturday Article' under the title 'Collections and Recollections'. Ransome was invited to take over and produce a weekly essay on any subject that took his fancy. On the face of it, this would be an

'In Rio Bay' by Clifford Webb for *Swallows and Amazons*.

'Making the Ship's Papers' by Clifford Webb.

The veteran 'steamer' *Tern* approaching Lakeside Pier in the spring of 2010 looks much as it did when Clifford Webb drew the vessel eighty years earlier.

The autumn glory of the Coniston fells seen across the lake from just south of Peel Island. The young Altounyans called the small islet Cormorant Island and who is to say that they were wrong?

The *Esperance* was the main model for Captain Flint's houseboat. This photograph shows the vessel at the time of *Swallows and Amazons* when it was owned by the Scott family. (courtesy Sir Oliver Scott)

In the 1930s only the *Esperance* had a mooring in the bay between Cockshot Point and the Ferry.

Arthur Ransome's sketch for the illustration of a cormorant in *Swallows and Amazons* is more accomplished than the entirely black drawing seen in the book.

treadmill, it is hardly surprising that progress with *Swallows and Amazons* was stifled. Fortunately, when Ted Scott, who had at last succeeded his father as editor, asked him at the end of November to go to Egypt again to cover the elections, Ransome took the book with him. He had continued to be plagued with his duodenal troubles, and when, just before Christmas, he was laid low with flu, he was able to forget all else for a few days and press on with the revision. Ransome was far from well when he returned at the beginning of February 1930, but this time he was determined to let nothing stand in the way of the book. His locum agreed to continue with the Saturday Articles for a few weeks while he completed the final manuscript. Cape wanted the Saturday Articles to form the second book of essays but Ransome was not interested, for he knew full well that his fate lay with *Swallows and Amazons*.

In April, Ransome went to Chichester to see Steven Spurrrier who had been commissioned to produce the maps and illustrations. Spurrier was a distinguished artist-illustrator and had produced some highly decorative working drawings. In one sense they were the perfect illustrations for the book, having captured just that spirit of romance that makes the book special, but it is easy to see why Ransome did not like them, for Spurrier's work has something to say about the children. He rejected them out of hand, much to the dismay of Wren Howard who had been given the task (often a thankless one) of looking after their new children's author. Howard made it quite clear the way he felt about Ransome's rejection and his letter shows how well he already knew his man.

*I am naturally very disturbed by the fact that you dislike the Illustrations, or most of them so much, though actually I am not altogether surprised. Personally I believe that most of them would look very much better when reduced and reproduced, but it seems to me that it is not the slightest use going on with even a selection from them when you don't really like any of them at all. Frankly, I don't really believe that any illustrations would please you and with that point of view I heartily sympathise. It is difficult enough to get an illustrator to draw pictures of purely fictitious characters and places but when it comes to trying*

easy matter and he accepted, and began his series 'Drawn at a Venture'. He soon found that having complete freedom was not the advantage that he had anticipated, and the compilation of a weekly 1,500-word essay would often require a week's work. Until mid-September he was also engaged upon the last few of the 182 'Rod and Line' essays. The *Rod and Line* collection was published in July. In Ransome's little-known *The Fisherman's Library* published in 1955 the preface by Tom Fort declared that *Rod and Line* was one of the half-dozen 'indispensable masterpieces'.

Once he had stepped onto the Saturday articles

Arthur Ransome by
Hilda Trefusis while he
was in Egypt in 1930.
(courtesy Abbot Hall)

to get a man to draw pictures of real children and real places which he has never seen, the task seems to me to be obviously impossible.

I am writing to Spurrier — obviously not a pleasant job — and will break it to him as gently as I can. I am afraid that by now he will have done most of the drawings and of course we shall have to pay him just the same fee as if we had used the drawings. Nothing less would be fair. I have also warned the printer that there will be no illustrations, which, from one point of view, will be an advantage because the book, as you know, is long.

Of course the absence of illustrations will almost certainly make the book more difficult to sell, to start with at any rate, and we shall have to try to make up for the lack of illustrations by a very intensive campaign to influence, if we can, the reviewers. Of course if a certain number of them can be persuaded to come forward and review the book and at length, the day will probably be won. I enclose proofs of the endpapers and map and hope to heaven you will like these. I believe that in this case you will be satisfied because at any rate, to my unpractised eye, both drawings seem to me intriguing and the right sort of stuff for the job.

Spurrier's splendid maps were approved and the fine swashbuckling vignette showing a seaman and a pirate appeared on the title page. The coloured map of the lake appeared as endpapers, and as they had no other images, the map was adapted to make an unusual and effective dust jacket.

By a strange coincidence the book was being printed by the Edinburgh firm of J.J.Gray for whom Ransome's late brother Geoffrey had

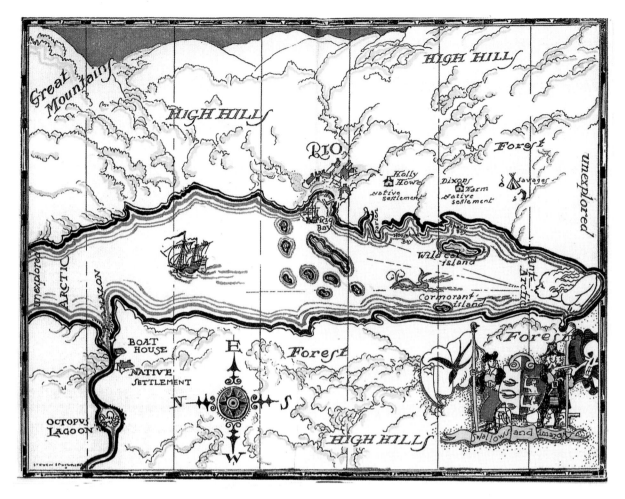

The lively endpaper map by Stephen Spurrier was used as a jacket for the first edition and truly caught the spirit of *Swallows and Amazons*.

worked, and was being given 'particular attention' in his memory. The proofs were ready at the beginning of June and were almost certainly corrected with his mother.

The book was dedicated to 'The six for whom it was written in exchange for a pair of slippers'. It seems that Ransome had a late change of mind for Spurrier's unused vignette says 'four'. Ransome was rather concerned about the Altounyans' reaction to their present, but he need not have fretted for there were cries of delight from Syria. Dora Altounyan wrote to say, '. . .we all like it *enormously*'. Titty wrote to say 'It is absolutely lovely and very exciting. I wish we had such lovely adventures as the Walkers had.' This was just

what he had hoped for, but he was most upset by Altounyan's sweeping assumptions, assuming the proud parent role, thinking what 'Damn fine sporting kids' he had and relishing his part as the author of the famous 'Duffer' telegram. Ransome was unprepared for such a simplistic reading and quick to realise that a game stops being a game when somebody begins to take things too seriously. Apparently, shortly before they had left for Aleppo, Altounyan had asked Ransome to write him a book that reminded him of the pleasures of sailing, and afterwards he claimed that to an extent he was instrumental in the creation of the book, and the story went round the family that Altounyan had asked Ransome why he did not put his children in a book. Whether or not this was so, Ransome certainly thought that he had taken too much on himself and his children. Relations between the two men deteriorated, as they grew older until Ransome refused to answer letters and would become upset if Altounyan's name were mentioned.

Early copies had been sent to family and friends, and on July 21st *Swallows and Amazons* was published. Several of Ransome's friends did their best for the book and among several favourable reviews there was one by Molly Hamilton for the literary journal *Time and Tide*.

*There is a small, a very small number of books designed for children which can be enjoyed by both children and grown-ups. Brer Rabbit, The Jungle Book, and Old Peter's Russian Tales are ones that spring to my mind: that fill the Bill, for me. Generally speaking, I dislike children's books most when they are meant for grown-ups. Mr. Ransome's new tale is not meant for grown-ups, but if I am any guide, lots of them will, nevertheless, like it a great deal. The only tinge of sadness that crosses my perfect enjoyment (I have read it twice already, by the way) is that born of the fact that I can't, now, enjoy the thrill open to the younger reader, who will, after reading, proceed to master the craft of sailing and set forth on wondrous and perilous adventures like John and Susan, Titty and Roger. They certainly will do that – and parents will send them forth to it, determined not to fall behind the mother and father of this delightful troupe of sea-men. Sea-men, one says – but the honours go to Able seaman Titty and to the dashing young ladies who manned the ship Amazon; enemies and rivals, at first; later sworn allies in the great campaign against Captain Flint, the master of the house-boat, owner of the parrot, and possessor of the treasure stolen from him – a theft of which Swallows are most unjustly suspected.*

*The action is genuinely exciting: with very real skill, Mr. Ransome has devised a mimic war whose incidents move with an absorbing tension. Even more attractive – at all events to the older reader – are the actors. Admirably characterized, the four Swallows do definitely belong to one family and at the same time stand out, perfectly individualized. They are more like one another than any one of them is like either of the Amazons, and that distinction, most delicately established, is held, right to the end. At the same time, they are quite distinct persons – the actions and speeches of Susan, for example, could never be confused with those of Titty. Titty, of course, is the star part; her experiences, alone on the island, like her heroic capture of the Amazons' boat, at a moment when it looks as though the battle between the two crews was helplessly lost, by Swallows (this reader, at any rate, is shamelessly on the side of Swallows), are the high points in the story; it is Titty, again, who finds the treasure on Cormorant Island, and restoring it to Captain Flint seals the friendship with which the great war on the houseboat closes. Titty is a delicious little person, and one hopes, greatly, to meet her again.*

*The other element that will fascinate both children and adults – the former unconsciously, the latter consciously – is the atmosphere of the book. The romance of a lake, fringed with trees, dotted with islands, steeps the whole book. It is nowhere set down in so many words; yet it pervades the whole atmosphere. One sees the sky and feels the breeze, the more acutely that they are, somehow, suggested, but never described. With the result that to read Swallows and Amazons is perfect escape from the here and now: in that sense a holiday, in itself.*

Once *Swallows and Amazons* was safely at the printers, Ransome decided that if it proved successful, his next book would be a rip-roaring adventure yarn in the Stevenson tradition, but before he could take the idea very far his publishers were calling for a sequel.

# Chapter Four

# SWALLOWDALE

ARTHUR RANSOME CELEBRATED the publication of *Swallows and Amazons* by fishing the River Leven estuary near Greenodd. As well as his adventure yarn he planned another collection of Russian fairy stories in case *Swallows and Amazons* should fail. Perhaps these were the Caucasian Folk Tales that he had planned in 1915. Evgenia had found several good ones that he liked, and he was hopeful that Cape would still be prepared to publish more 'Old Peter' tales instead of those essays. Instead he fell ill. There had been plenty to worry about that summer, because apart from the financial uncertainty of his future, he was desperately anxious about the book's reception.

The Harley Street specialist that he consulted, Dr F.C.E. Danvers-Atkinson diagnosed duodenal or gastric ulcers, foretold a long cure and forbad smoking. Meanwhile there was still a crust to earn and he had to give Ivy around a third of the loaf. His resignation from the staff of the *Manchester Guardian* had ensured that he could remain in England, but Cape's £100 advance was not due until the end of September, and it would be months before the sales of *Swallows and Amazons* would reach a figure that would bring in royalties. There were still occasional requests for books to review and leaders to write for the *Manchester Guardian* and the *Observer*. Some of these were composed from his sickbed in Molly Hamilton's London flat while she was in America, to which she had been consigned, subsisting on Danvers-Atkinson's prescribed diet of bismuth and milk at two-hourly intervals. It was many years since Ransome had been in London for any length of time and he was cheered on his road to recovery by a whole string of old friends who called each

evening and he freely admitted he had thoroughly enjoyed that part of being ill. By September he was rejoicing that after five weeks of bismuth he was allowed some toast on condition that he chewed it thoroughly.

At the beginning of October he was heartened by a letter from his old mentor, W.G. Collingwood.

*...I have today re-read Swallows and Amazons and enjoyed it ever so much. Somehow you have made your Titty so very like my Titty: and in a degree your Ruth-Nancy is more like my Ruth [his granddaughter Ursula Ruth Collingwood] than could be expected unless you had seen her here last month being a savage with a woodland lair, which was quite realistic. Unfortunately we lost Titty to join her parents, and they frizzle out for want of support; but she is a true pirate at heart!*

*I'm most sorry for your continued illness, but I live in hope of seeing you recovered. And perhaps the Blacketts and Walkers will do some more lively things: they are too good a crew to be dismissed in a hurry.*

The following month brought the news that Cape had arranged for *Swallows and Amazons* to be published in America by the Philidelphia firm of J.B. Lippencott and that a substantial quantity would be taken by an American book club — The Junior Literary Guild. Ransome was in a buoyant mood when he returned to Low Ludderburn to do some gentle fishing. 'Three cheers for the Stars and Stripes!' he rejoiced.

Ransome had no intention of dismissing the Blacketts and the Walkers, but for a time he had thought in terms of involving them in a wild fantasy of pirates and buried treasure. He enjoyed writing the opening pages that he considered better than the beginning of *Swallows and Amazons* but Cape made it clear that they wanted a sequel to *Swallows and Amazons* and he was not to bother with anything else,

There were further celebrations that month when it was reported that *Swallows and Amazons* had received the royal approval, but Ransome could not help remembering that John had remarked that he had no time for queens! Her Majesty had gone shopping in the famous Oxford Street bookshop John & Edward Bumpus and bought a copy. 'She paid cash! I asked.' Within a

In *Swallowdale* Arthur Ransome describes the boatbuilders' sheds in Rio Bay in detail. Sadly, these were pulled down many years ago and the southern part of the bay changed for ever.

few years Bumpus would be taking large stocks of the latest Ransome for the Christmas market.

Writing was brought to an end by a second collapse and recurrence of the agonies that had made him seek help from Dr Danvers-Atkinson. This time he wisely sought a second opinion from Dr Forest Smith of St Thomas's Hospital, who took x-rays, conducted further tests and confirmed the diagnosis. He also recommended a bland, milk-based diet, but advised Ransome, who was down to ten stone by then, to put on weight until he was around 15 stone. Furthermore, he condemned aluminium cooking utensils and told Ransome to be sure to avoid their use — and for the rest of his life Evgenia saw to it that he always did. She also saw to it that her husband was never without a small bottle of milk and some biscuits that he carried around in a small suitcase.

They returned to Ludderburn before Christmas and slowly Ransome's condition improved, though he continued to be in pain until well into 1931 and from time to time for the rest of his life. By the time he was able to turn his attention to Cape's follow-up, he knew that *Swallows and Amazons* had created a demand for another Lake Country novel and this had to be satisfied before he could begin his 'Treasure Island' fantasy.

Ransome had a vague idea in mind when he went to tea with the Kelsalls. That afternoon, Desmond went down to Hartbarrow Bridge to meet him.

*Walking back from the bridge Arthur Ransome asked if I had enjoyed* Swallows and Amazons. *I said, yes, very much, and was he going to write*

Rio Bay with the boatmen's huts in the foreground and the Victorian boatsheds beyond the pier.

The Blawith Swallowdale looking down the valley from the upper waterfall.

From the summit cairn of Beacon Fell there is a fine view of the whole of the High Moor country looking towards the distant slopes of Kanchenjunga and the valley of the Amazon.

The Scafells seen from the summit of Coniston Old Man (Kanchenjunga) on an unforgettable May day almost forty years ago.

Swallowdale by Helene Carter.

another to follow it?

*Arthur Ransome said that he was thinking about it. Supposing that he did, what did I think ought to happen in it? With a small boy's typical lack of inhibition I said that I thought that John should become over-confident in handling Swallow and should run her on the rocks. Arthur Ransome gave a great guffaw of laughter and said, 'That's exactly what I was thinking myself, but I haven't got any further than that at the moment.'*

When Ransome was preparing the Ship's Papers for Swallowdale the Kelsall brothers signed for John and Roger and arranged for their parrot to provide the imprint of Polly's claws.

On the first page of handwritten notes for the story Captain Flint and the Amazons are putting up two new tents for the Swallows on Wild Cat Island. The date is given as August 3rd. Later that morning the Swallows arrive and are greeted with the sad news of the Great Aunt's arrival at Beckfoot that will mean that the Amazons cannot camp until after she has left. After a discussion Captain Flint goes home and the rest sail to Horseshoe Cove to start where they left off last summer. While their elders are content to remain in the cove, Titty and Roger explore and come across a secret valley. They hurry back to tell the others to find everybody ready to go home. The Amazons explain that they have to stay at home next day, but the day after they will sail down to the Cove early in the morning.

The following day the Swallows make their early morning visit to Dixon's Farm and settle down to island life once more. The day after that, when the Amazons are seen sailing down to Horseshoe Cove in the early morning, the Swallows start their day with bathing and breakfast. *Swallow* and her crew follow and at 9.30 the little boat is wrecked. Working together, they manage to raise the wreck and bring it ashore. Peggy, Titty and Roger go off for milk while the others put a patch over the damage.

On the fourth day, they decide that *Swallow* can make the passage to Holly Howe under jury rig with the *Amazon* in convoy, but Captain Flint aboard the houseboat sees them, and rows out to tell John to sail straight for Rio. At Borwicks *Swallow* is handed over to the boatbuilders before Captain Flint takes John to Holly Howe, but leaves him in the rowing boat to watch from the distance while he talks to Mother.

The Swallows have clearly been given leave to camp beside the Cove, for on the fifth day Titty and Roger lead an expedition to the secret valley. On the way back they see the Amazons in their best frocks sitting opposite Mrs Blackett and the Great Aunt in an open carriage. The Swallows are shocked by what they have just seen. Even Roger sees nothing to laugh at. Next day they move camp to the secret valley and on the seventh day of their holiday make a bathing pool, and there the planning ends.

On another page there are some ideas jotted down. The episode of the hound trail coming through the camp, Roger's sprained ankle and his improvised stretcher, the holiday tasks, Titty's cave and Mother's visit to the camp, all were worked into the story.

In Swallowdale the shipwrecked Swallows briefly consider becoming savages, an echo of the possibilities that occurred to the author in the early stages of planning. There is a mention of a tribe and their carved totem to which offerings are made. Perhaps Nancy and Peggy would make a surprise attack, capture the totem and make off with Titty in hot pursuit. Or the Tribe would arrive in camp to find their totem gone — an episode that would find its way into Secret Water. The final note says simply, 'Beacon fire'. Katherine Hull and Pamela Whitlock would make good use of flaming beacons in the night sky in *The Far Distant Oxus*.

The setting for the secret valley seems to be in the Beacon Fell area, west of Coniston Water. Here there is Beacon Tarn — a lovely inspiration for Trout Tarn, a valley with a knickerbockerbreaker, a waterfall and a look out rock, and a beck winding its way through the bracken and heather.

In his desk diary for each year, beginning with 1931, Ransome created a chart on which he entered the number of pages written or revised each day, the total for the month and the grand total, and the

Peter Duck's cave by Helene Carter

day that he posted the manuscript to Cape. Sometimes in a period when he was not writing he would enter the reason — 'Broads', 'London' or at work on the pictures and so on. Five pages was a fair day's work when he was writing the first draft, ten a very good one. Revision varied from book to book; *Peter Duck* went so easily that for a time he completed between 15 and 20 pages each day.

By the time that Ransome began to write the first draft at the beginning of January, he had let on to his American publisher about 'The Shipwrecked Swallows' or 'The Camp in Swallowdale'. 'I've provided a really good shipwreck and the rest of the book

Dow Crag from the summit of Coniston Old Man (Kanchenjunga) beyond which lies the sea and the rarely seen Isle of Man.

Coniston Water with Peel Island just visible in the distance, viewed from the upper slopes of the Old Man.

Beyond Coppermines Valley above the village of Coniston, the track runs beside the Levers Water beck making it a likely spot for the Swallows half-way camp.

After leaving the Amazons at Watersmeet, the Swallows climbed up past the waterfalls towards their half-way camp on Kanchenjunga.

follows on naturally.' He had originally planned that before climbing Kanchenjunga (Coniston Old Man), the Swallows would follow the River Amazon to its source. That idea was discarded in favour of 'The Noon-tide Owl' and 'The Half-way Camp'.

Ransome had taken a bold step in putting the most dramatic episode in the book — the wreck of the *Swallow* — in chapter five, followed by 31 chapters in which the plot meanders towards the happy return to Wild Cat Island with *Swallow* mended, the Great Aunt gone and the possibility that anything could happen in the next fortnight.

Once started, Ransome progressed with a great rush of enthusiasm that carried him through more than 80 pages by January 18th. However he had rather unwisely set himself to see if he could average 10 pages a day and at one point he noted with horror that he was 17 pages behind schedule! A month later he had 152 pages of rough copy, as far as the completion of the Swallows overland trek to the Amazon River.

Meanwhile he had admired the illustrations that Helene Carter had drawn for the American edition of *Swallows and Amazons* and had written a warm letter of appreciation to Ernestine Evans of Lippencott. ('I think your Helene Carter must be a most charming person.') Unlike Stephen Spurrier who put the children centre stage, in illustrating *Swallowdale*, Helene Carter created a romantic landscape that dwarfs the tiny figures of the children. Turning to his own work, he confided that he hoped to build up a 'regular row' of these books, and that he had a very different story in mind that would one day become his best book.'

In April, the first copies of the American edition arrived and Ransome sent one to his daughter. Tabitha was now almost 20 years of age — too old to enjoy the book as a child and probably too young to appreciate it as an adult. She wrote to say that she had been unable to finish the book and her letter depressed Ransome rather more than perhaps it should, and the writing of *Swallowdale* stalled for a fortnight.

More cheering was the news that by the beginning of March Cape had sold more than three-quarters of the 2000 copies of *Swallows and Amazons*. The publishers regarded this more favourably than its author who had set himself a target of annual sales of 3000. Cape announced a new illustrated edition would be published in September and had commissioned an artist called Clifford Webb to produce 30 full-page illustrations and numerous vignettes. After Ransome's approval of Helene Carter's illustrations there was real hope at Cape's that Webb would be able to please him as she had done.

Towards the end of March and in early April the book progressed so well that he had completed the first draft before the arrival of Clifford Webb. Webb stayed at Low Ludderburn for four days making sketches. He was well thought of as an artist, but was comparatively new to book illustration. Ransome sailed *Swallow* round Belle Isle and back and forth across Bowness Bay while Webb made a number of drawings of the little boat. Webb drew the houseboat *Esperance* in the bay north of the Ferry and sailed in *Swallow* down Windermere to Blake Holme. The following day they went to Coniston where Webb sketched Bank Ground Farm, and Ransome borrowed *Mavis* from the Lanehead boathouse and took him to Peel Island. Anyone looking for the features that inspired the enchanted landscape of *Swallows and Amazons* and *Swallowdale* can do no better than begin with a study of Webb's illustrations. There is a topographical faithfulness of the stylish full-page illustrations that seem almost exclusively of Coniston Water, Peel Island and the surrounding area — apart from the depictions of Rio, Horseshoe Cove and the houseboat. There are a number of very fine illustrations as Ransome freely admitted, and all have an attractive style of their own. Webb used his children Michael and Jennifer as models, but if there is a weakness in the illustrations it is the rather stiff appearance of the explorers and pirates. Webb had been wounded in the First World War and he received a disability pension, but when he bumped *Swallow* making a clumsy pierhead jump, it was never forgotten, any more than the banana skin that Taqui Altounyan once left on the deck of *Nancy Blackett*. The Ransomes failed to hit it off with their guest, and his dislike of Webb probably coloured Ransome's private criticism of Webb's work that he felt had failed to capture the spirit and character of the scene, although he was very complimentary to Webb himself.

Ransome's resignation from the *Manchester Guardian* had done nothing to weaken his friendship with Ted Scott who had been overworking for years, and after much persuasion on Ransome's part, they hired a pair of Broads cruising yachts. Their craft, the *Welcome* and

*Winsome* were 20 feet in length but with only five feet of headroom, and were described as a distinctive, fast single cabin yachts specially designed for newcomers and for single-handed sailing. Scott and his son Dick were beginners, and it was with great pleasure that Ransome saw how well they took to sailing. Both went overboard and got out without fuss — an incident that would appear in *Coot Club*. Evgenia managed to crack Ransome on the head with the boom, but otherwise their cruise along the northern rivers was delightful.

On their return to Ludderburn Ransome had a first look at Webb's drawings, and he had to admit that they were 'really very good'. Then he settled to a complete revision and worked steadily through most of May. The beginning of the book gave him the most trouble and having reread his revision he dismissed the first chapter in one word — 'Tosh!'

Once the Swallows have become established in the secret valley that had now acquired a hidden cave, they become friendly with the natives at the nearby farm, are taught to catch trout by Captain Flint and they begin their holiday tasks, before the Amazons are able to make their next appearance in a promised surprise attack. Spotted by Titty, the Swallows' lookout, the Amazons are outwitted by their disappearance into the cave. The Amazons' departure is delayed by staying to watch a hound trail that passes through the valley and they do not arrive home until after supper, having promised to be back for mid-day dinner. Hardly surprisingly, they have to remain with the family until the Great Aunt has gone. John is at work on a new mast in Horseshoe Cove one day when Nancy secretly fires an arrow into the mouth of the cove from the

IN HORSESHOE COVE

**Clifford Webb's illustration 'In Horseshoe Cove' for *Swallowdale*.**

passing Beckfoot launch. Cunningly fitted in the arrow is a message that sends the Swallows trekking across the moor to Beckfoot where they meet the Amazons who have managed to escape for an hour or two. Nancy plans to lead them to the summit of Kanchenjunga the following morning to celebrate the Great Aunt's departure. Modern readers may wonder why Coniston Old Man was renamed Kanchenjunga rather than Everest, but in the early nineteen-thirties Kanchenjunga expeditions were making headline news. The explorers arrange to meet the Amazons the following morning half way up the mountain where the Swallows are to spend the night. After the

Arthur Ransome's flags are held by the Abbot Hall Museum together with many of his belongings. The swallow flag is rectangular like that shown in the drawings by Clifford Webb. (courtesy Abbot Hall)

Looking down the waterfall at the entrance to a Swallowdale valley among the Blawith fells.

The great rock at the entrance to a Swallowdale valley among the Blawith Fells. After rain, the water tumbles over the top of the rock and pours down the steep slope. The place has a striking resemblance to Clifford Webb's illustration.

The rear of Low Yewdale Farm (Dixon's Farm) has the feeling of the illustrations by both Clifford Webb and Arthur Ransome.

Seen from the top of the Swallowdale waterfall, the cove where the beck enters the lake looks remarkably like the Clifford Webb illustration 'In Horseshoe Cove'.

'The Charcoal Burners' Hut' by Clifford Webb.

they discover that *Swallow* has been repaired and is waiting in there, and Captain Flint suggests a race. In the earlier outline John tires of Nancy's boasting about *Amazon*'s speed and issues a challenge, but this would not have been true to Nancy's character, for whatever flaws that she may have and for all her bossiness, she is not given to boasting.

In a short exchange that never appeared in the book, she showed the understanding side of her nature when Peggy asks why she let John steer *Amazon* during their sail down to Horseshoe Cove. 'Don't you see, you donkey,' she replies. 'He's lost his ship and if I hadn't he'd have thought I didn't trust him with *Amazon*.'

During the race, John's trick of lifting the keel over the shallows thereby saving a tack and winning the race, was something that Ernest Altounyan had done on one occasion.

The race ends at Beckfoot where Mrs Walker and Bridget join them in a feast. Sailing back to Horseshoe Cove in company they are horrified to see smoke rising from Wild Cat Island. They land in the harbour and storm the camp, only to find Captain Flint has brought all their camping things down from the secret valley.

'Pouf!' said Susan raking the sticks together in the fireplace. 'Isn't it a blessing to get home?'

The early part of the book continued to give him trouble. At one point he all but decided that the book should open with the shipwreck. On July 2nd he vented his frustration in his diary: 'Read 'Jury Rig' to Genia. vvv bad. Much scrapped. This means rewriting three chapters and rearranging the story. Better let Captain Flint share in patching the boat.'

To help him prepare the

conquest of the mountain, Titty and Roger set off to follow the trail of pine cones to Swallowdale while John and Susan take passage in *Amazon*. The younger ones become lost in the fog and Roger sprains his ankle close to where the charcoal burners are working and Young Billy says that he must remain while Titty is given a lift to Swallowdale.

Ransome had originally intended to kill off Old Billy during the winter, so as to leave room in the hut for the wounded man, but Ransome must have felt that this might upset younger readers, so the old fellow was packed off to lord it over a nearby hound trail instead.

Next morning Roger is collected and returns to Swallowdale on an improvised stretcher. Mother and Bridget visit Swallowdale and when they go down to the cove to see them off illustrations, Ransome had sent Webb a draft of the first eight chapters on June 20th and he sent the rest in chunks as it was typed. He was still not satisfied with the first two chapters, and these were revised during a visit to London in the middle of July, so that the first chapter starts with the Swallows sailing to Wild Cat Island with no signs of the Amazons and the houseboat shut up. Finally, on July 29th the typescript went to the printer and Ransome wrote triumphantly in his diary the single word, 'Done!'

The proofs arrived at the end of August and Ransome took them to his mother who was now living back in Leeds so that they might go through them together. He was better in health, and more cheerful, since the book was completed, but desperately needing confirmation that the book was all right. It came from Cape when Wren Howard wrote to say that they liked it better than *Swallows and Amazons* and that it would be published at the end of October, a month after the illustrated edition of *Swallows and Amazons* and just in time for the Christmas market. The print run would be 2000 copies, the same as Swallows and Amazons.

Dora Altounyan took a sympathetic view of Clifford Webb's work when she received the new edition of *Swallows and Amazons*, and she wrote to say that, on the whole she did not think that she could have done them much better.

*... the things that the illustrations fall short on are the things that nobody knows except us, the secret japes and details that your general public doesn't know anything about. Of course the kind of illustrations that YOU IMAGINE I could have made (though I myself am perfectly sure I could never have done them) would have made a 'perfect book' more perfect still, and I do most awfully wish I could have done it.*

*We are simply LONGING for Swallowdale.*

Just before publication, Ransome sent copies to his friends and the response that probably meant most to him was from W.G.Collingwood, at that time a very ill man who managed to write, 'I have been hard at work reading *Swallowdale* ever since getting it and I find it quite as good as S&A. I cannot say fairer than that. Good luck to the book and its author.'

*In Swallowdale* Ransome comes closest to writing about his own childhood holidays. Roger slides down a steeply sloping rock that Titty names the knickerbockerbreaker and has his trousers darned by Mary Swainson at the nearby farm, exactly as his creator had done forty years before.

*Swallowdale* was reviewed by Naomi Mitchison for the *Spectator*. After bewailing the glut of imitation books flooding the Christmas market that year, she goes on:

*Swallowdale is a real book. Probably most children with sensible parents have already had its predecessor, Swallows and Amazons. I think the new one is even better than the old, and the illustrations are admirable, both as showing what happened to John, Susan and the others, and as pictures. It is the kind of book that one discusses in the upper forms of preparatory schools, or even in the lower forms of public schools. It is realer than any of the old children's 'classics' seem now; these boys and girls are far more competent, intelligent and kind than any Victorian or Edwardian family; they have infinitely more dignity and sense of purpose, without having lost either in imagination or adventurousness; they are, in fact, real, modern children, and those who feel gloomy about the future of England should consider that it is boys and girls like the Swallows and Amazons who are the potential new citizens — and there is little to fear! But the main body of readers — those from nine to fourteen — will appreciate it straightforwardly as an account of adventures to people like themselves, possible, solid, completely satisfying adventures on what must have been the best of all summer holidays.*

In October letters began to arrive from Aleppo. Taqui Altounyan said forthrightly, '*Swallowdale* is even better than *Swallows and Amazons* and you needn't have been so pessimistic about it. . . . . I love that part where Titty does the wax image stunt and when the Amazons usually much more efficient than the Swallows, forgot to take off their red caps.'

She was not without some criticisms,

*I don't care what you say, we all think Capt Flint is exactly like you — is you, in fact. The Ship's Baby says she can make a much better B than the one on the ship's papers and we can all write our names without those artificial looking blots.*

The early copies of the book seem to have contained some image reversal, because she goes on,

*Those headpieces upside down don't really matter much, anyway, they are so bad that they couldn't look much better the right way up. The only good picture is the one of the Amazons not in pirate rig driving with the GA. I do wish the best of all natives would do the illustrations.*

Titty Altounyan was equally enthusiastic, 'I have finished reading *Swallowdale,* and I think it is just as good — if not better than *Swallows and Amazons.* I would love to have adventures like that.' Titty always felt that her namesake was a much more gifted and capable person than she was, and she continued, 'I can't imagine how I swam with the telescope. The other day I tried putting both my hands above my head and swimming but I only went under. I do wish you will come soon and write another book.'

As she grew older, the connection became something of a burden. Titty had joined in Ransome's game, partly to please him, so that even when she wrote to him from boarding school she still signed herself 'Titty A. B.', but she felt a fraud and was too polite to tell him so. 'I loved Uncle Arthur and Aunt Genia. They were nice, kind, exciting and interesting people and I never stopped loving them.'

Titty's wish came true the following spring when the Ransomes went out to Syria while he was hard at work on *Peter Duck*.

A few colliers still burn charcoal using traditional methods in various parts of the country. This preserved or reconstructed hut was seen in Grizedale Forest some years ago.

The charcoal pudding waiting to be covered with clods of turf and soaked with water.

During the descent of Kanchenjunga, Nancy allowed the explorers to use the spiralling footpath, admitting that it was quicker.

The channel behind Long Island chosen by John in the race with *Amazon* in *Swallowdale*.

# Chapter Five

# PETER DUCK

IN HER BOOK *Arthur Ransome and Captain Flint's Trunk*, Christina Hardyment published the two chapters of Ransome's early draft of *Peter Duck*. He gave it the title 'Their Own Story', and it takes place during the Christmas holidays following the adventures in *Swallows and Amazons*. The explorers, pirates, and Captain Flint are together again on board a wherry yacht, the *Polly Ann*, on the Broads during a hard winter. When the yacht becomes frozen in, 'Their Own Story' takes off when Nancy is dismissive of *Swallows and Amazons* and claims that Captain Flint could not have written it, because if he were telling a story it would be something a lot more exciting. They remember how they sat in Nancy and Peggy's tent during the storm and told each other the story of their shipwreck, and begin to make up a story about their voyage aboard a schooner. Peter Duck makes an appearance in the second chapter as the *Polly Ann's* paid hand. He joins in the storytelling and it is he who names their schooner 'Wild Cat'. The *Wild Cat* is fleeing down Channel under full sail when the draft ends without explaining the reason for their haste.

Even in the draft, Ransome captures the feeling of the Broads in winter in his best manner. The story opens, '"The light's burning all right but the fog's as thick as ever," said Titty shutting the door of the cabin quickly behind her, but not quickly enough to stop a cold breath from outside and a soft cloud of fog from slipping through into the warm lamplight of the cabin.'

At the beginning of October 1931, Ransome returned to the drudgery of the weekly articles for the *Manchester Guardian* with a piece called 'Tock Tock!' and continued with such as 'If I Were a Piano

. . .'. In the New Year, after Ted Scott had reduced his fee from seven to six guineas — a necessary economy due to the recession, he wrote his final Saturday article, 'Last Year's Notebooks'. Ivor Brown took over on a permanent basis the following week when the Ransomes set off for Syria.

Ransome had already resolved that his next book would be about a former Baltic trading schooner *Wild Cat* and the old seaman from *Racundra*, when letters began to arrive from Aleppo. After telling him that she thought that his next book should be about an island with hidden treasure that the Swallows should find after having lots of adventures, Titty Altounyan went on,

*...Mummy says if you want to write another book about us, you had better come here and see what we are really like, because you know we are all two years older than when you saw us last, and if you did that you would be able to write a book that is really like us.*

*For instance, if you stayed with us in summer in Souk-a-look you would camp with us and see how we build nests in trees and track wild boar etc. This is Mummy's idea. Please do come here, it would be lovely, and bring Aunt Genia too.*

Taqui Altounyan was equally persuasive and added a request that he bring with him a 10 foot sailing dinghy,

*Hurry up and make Swallow snug for the winter, fill a hundred coconuts with food for the birds, put a notice on Low Ludderburn gate saying 'TO LET FOR A YEAR' and jump from an express train onto an express steamer and from these onto an express car or on to a camel and you'll be here in no time. And mind you bring the 10- footer . . .*

Ernest Altounyan was even more demanding, saying that as well as the dinghy for which he sent £20 as part-payment, would Ransome bring a Broads wherry with two quants! Until almost the last moment they remained undecided whether to make the visit. On the one hand it would be good to see Dora and the children again, but on the other the cost of the journey would eat up what was left of their meagre savings. Altounyan, tiring of the uncertainty, wrote accusing Ransome of having no intention of coming to stay, and of 'playing fast and loose with us Swallows'. More persuasive however, was his confidence that he could work a final cure with Ransome's ulcer that was still giving him 'corkscrews' of pain in the solar plexus from time to time.

They were seen off at Salford Docks by Ted Scott on January 8th 1932 and sailed the following day. Evgenia noticed that the two men spoke of nothing but sailing, for Scott was becoming as committed to sailing as Ransome. They arranged another Easter cruise on the Broads when the Ransomes returned, and meanwhile Scott was going to look at the dinghy with buoyancy tanks that Ransome had recommended. If suitable, his son, Dick and he were planning to do some sailing on Windermere.

Their ship was the *Scottish Prince* that was trading between Manchester and Alexandria at that time. The journey out was hugely enjoyable, in spite of the restrictions of their tiny cabin and Ransome's fear that the ship was so lightly loaded that they would roll abominably. The new dinghy built in Burnham on Crouch was safely stowed in the ship's hold. They were sorely tempted to put the little craft in the water when they berthed in Malta but in the end decided against taking it from its packing case. After a week afloat, Ransome was feeling perfectly well and was able to join in deck games. He took a copy of *Treasure Island* on the voyage and he borrowed a copy of *The Channel Pilot* from which he took notes that he thought would come in useful, although he did not actually start the book on the voyage.

After calling at Tunis and Malta, the *Scottish Prince* docked at Alexandria on January 24th. They transferred to a Greek Khedivial mail boat, the Belkas, shifting their luggage and the large wooden packing case containing the precious dinghy from one ship to another with difficulty. The *Belkas* wandered around the Mediterranean for a week before they were able to disembark at Alexandretta on February 1st, arriving in Aleppo the same day.

Three days later Ransome started *Peter Duck*. In her memoir *Chimes from a Wooden Bell*, Taqui Altounyan recalls that every morning Ransome retired to her mother's room at the top of the house and worked until he heard the dinner gong. At the time he seemed convinced that the book was a failure and cast down by Evgenia's verdict that it was awful.

The new book was a strange mixture. The tale was pure swashbuckling romance, yet the time was the present and the cast of Swallows and Amazons was firmly rooted in reality. There are some echoes of *Treasure Island*, although Black Jake is no Long John Silver and it is the old seaman, Peter Duck, who remains in the memory. Readers who came to *Peter Duck* after reading S*wallowdale* had been prepared for the 'rattling good yarn' that the Swallows and Amazons and Captain Flint had made up, in which they voyage to the Caribbees and come back with their pockets 'full of pirate gold'. Ransome knew what he was about and the book proved an immediate success.

Peter Duck, Black Jake, his villainous crew and the red-haired boy Bill belong to a romantic world that Ransome created and into which Captain Flint and the children have strayed in their storytelling game. When the pursuing pirate ship comes alongside the *Wild Cat* in the dark there is real menace, yet Captain Flint's reply, 'Haul your wind, or, by crumbs, I'll sink your ship,' is the stuff of play. The villains are drowned, Peter Duck is laid out, Bill has his arm broken and loses some teeth, but the Swallows and Amazons are kept at arm's length from the pirates.

Ransome enjoyed developing the character of Peter Duck, the unflappable, philosophical and down-to-earth old seaman and he thought that his red-haired boy Bill was great fun. Readers of *Racundra's First Cruise* would recognise in Peter Duck, the 'Ancient Mariner' Carl Sehmel, *Racundra*'s crew — 'He was a very little man with a white beard and a head as bald as my own. Sometimes on board he wore a crimson stocking-cap with a tassel, when he looked like a gnome, a pixey or a fairy cobbler. If Queen Mab went to sea she could not find a fitter mariner.'

Crab Island was inspired by the real-life uninhabited island of Trinidad off the coast of Brazil, where a hoard, including gold candlesticks from the cathedral of Lima, was reputed to have been buried in 1821 during the American War of Independence. The tale of his unsuccessful treasure-hunting expedition of 1889 was told in E.F. Knight's *The Cruise of the Alerte* and inspired not only Ransome but also John Masefield, whose book, *The Midnight Folk* is concerned with the missing Santa Barbara treasure. Both Trinidad and Crab Island were volcanic and infested by land crabs. 'The loathsome land crabs might well be the restless spirit of the pirates themselves, for they are indeed more ugly and evil and generally more diabolical-looking than the bloodiest pirate who ever lived,' reported Knight.

While they were in Aleppo they received the first copies of the American edition of *Swallowdale*, and Ransome was disgusted to find that the first chapter had been 'cut to pieces and spoilt by the omission of the last three sentences. VERY DAMN INDEED.'

Ransome wrote every day for the first eight days in Aleppo and had covered 57 pages, breaking off only to join the others at the launching of the little dinghy that they had decided should be called *Peter Duck*. By the end of February the total had reached 117 pages, and when they left Aleppo in April, Ransome had 310 pages completed. From time to time he read passages of the yarn to various members of the family and so was able to gauge different people's reactions. Since the book was supposed to be the work of children, it had been agreed that he would illustrate it himself. As it turned out, this was not quite accurate, as he told his mother, 'Titty A.B. is working hard helping to produce pictures for the new book. She is most comically like her imaginary self. Ditto Roger.'

It would be wrong to dismiss the visit as a failure. Both Arthur and Evgenia enjoyed their time with the children, and he had found the high workroom with its view over the street below and its camels, donkeys and high-spirited Arabs passing by, very congenial. On the down side he had arrived in good health, and by April was much bothered by his duodenals and fearful that he would develop malaria (Evgenia hated having to sleep under a mosquito net). Some tension had developed towards the end of the visit and there were stand-up rows that had to be patched up afterwards. Dora had been educated at home and was teaching her children, but times had changed, and both Ransome and Evgenia — particularly Evgenia — thought the four oldest should be sent to England and school. Looking back as an adult, Taqui saw that both Evgenia and her father were people who had to get their own way with the inevitable result.

So far as the children were concerned, the Ransomes left in mid-April without any warning. It was a tearful departure, for they had grown very fond of Ukatha, and having no children of their own, it had been a novel experience for Arthur and Evgenia, as they joinied in the children's daily game of tennis and entertained them in the evening by singing, playing the penny whistle or telling Anansi stories.

They were able to catch up with the *Scottish Prince* in Cyprus en route to Amsterdam. The return voyage was as pleasant as the outward one and once Ransome's health improved, he was able to press on with *Peter Duck*. By the time they docked in Amsterdam he had added a further 46 pages. On arrival they received the news that Ted Scott had died in a boating accident on Windermere. Ransome took it very badly, feeling that he had been responsible for his friend's death, as it was he who had introduced Scott and his son to sailing. Evgenia recorded, 'Ted's death the most terrible blow that fate could have dealt us'.

After three days in London, Evgenia travelled north alone, while Ransome went to Lowestoft to collect some local colour. Arriving at Low Ludderburn, she found that the cottage had been burgled and left open, letting in mice and damp. Nothing, other than food, had been taken, but it was a most unpleasant homecoming.

It was three weeks before Ransome could bring himself to settle to *Peter Duck*, but once he started, he forged ahead and on June 4th he was able to begin the revision. The book opens with the schooner *Wild Cat* fitting out in Lowestoft harbour. Another schooner across the harbour is also preparing for a long voyage, and the Swallows fall foul of her piratical skipper, Black Jake, even before they are actually aboard the *Wild Cat*. The old seaman Peter Duck joins the crew of the *Wild Cat* and soon the little green schooner is off down Channel and eventually voyaging to the Caribbean island where Peter Duck had secretly witnessed treasure being buried when he was a lad. Black Jake is also set on finding the treasure and follows *Wild Cat* to Crab Island, arriving just as the treasure has been revealed amongst the wreckage after a violent storm hits the island. He gives chase, bent on capturing the *Wild Cat* and seizing the treasure, only to be foiled when a waterspout strikes his ship.

Practically all that remains of any working notes to indicate how Ransome developed the plot is a few scribbled lines, setting the scene as Black Jake and the crew of the *Viper* finally catch up with the *Wild Cat* becalmed in the Sargasso Sea. Both ships drift for days within sight of each other, before the Vipers take to the boats, and armed to the teeth with knives prepare to board.

Some more clues can be found in the letter written by Taqui Altounyan shortly after the Ransomes arrived in England.

*I'm sorry I didn't come and wave a damp hanky at you when you drove off. Mine was certainly damp but I was feeling too much of a donk to wave it. Sorry — anyway, we'll go on to more pleasant subjects. No, wait a sec. What rotten bad luck that you had to chuck that chapter about calm in mid-Atlantic. Couldn't you say that the waters were not shark-infested? But you need not cut the whole thing out, there could still be a calm and the crew plus captains etc could drop bits of meat (not human) overboard and watch for sharks and if any come to get them, then PD could tell his yarn about being towed by a shark. Anyway I hope that awful man hasn't told you anything else that necessitates you pitching out a few more beloved pages.*

Reviewing his draft, Ransome thought that three chapters in the middle needed attention and the beginning required a complete re-write, otherwise he thought it ought to be plain sailing. Once started, the revision forged ahead. In the last four days of June alone, he completed 53 pages and the book was finished a month later and sent off. Never again would revision be so straightforward. Producing illustrations was a different proposition. Taqui Altounyan went on:

*How are you getting on with the pictures, or are you going to give up and dispatch a telegram to Helene Carter asking her to come and stay with you and see what a real-live boat looks like? I think that would be the best plan if you get desperate.*

Had it been at all practicable, that is exactly what Ransome would have liked. His mother was a fine amateur watercolourist, the Collingwoods were art school trained (in 1989 the Abbott Hall Gallery in Kendal held a retrospective of Dora Altounyan's paintings), and these were the standards by which he judged his own work. Making the carefully inked drawings for reproduction would have been a much more pleasurable task but for the caustic comments of Evgenia, whose verdict ranged from 'passable' to 'disgraceful'.

Almost 20 of Ransome's sketchbooks and tiny notebooks containing miniatures have survived,

**Arthur Ransome's pencil drawing of Kyrenia in Cyprus made on their return from Aleppo, 1932.**

together with loose drawings and paintings, inked master drawings for the illustrations, embellished letters to his mother, his daughter Tabitha and his publisher, and a number of handmade Christmas cards showing sailing boats that he sent to friends. As well as the many sketches recognisable as preparatory work for the illustrations, there are drawings and paintings made for his own pleasure. These include drawings and watercolours of landscapes, flower studies and portraits. The sketchbooks also contain sketches by his mother and possibly Dora and Barbara. One tantalising page shows a girl wearing two sorts of stocking cap with a tassel drawn from nine different angles and is certainly not the work of Ransome.

Perhaps illustrating *Peter Duck* was not quite such an unwelcome task as Ransome made out. Calling in a leading London bookshop to see how well *Swallows and Amazons* was selling he was told that it had made a good start but that it was a pity that there were no pictures; attractive pictures by a recognised artist were almost essential if a book was to do at all well. 'An artist would be sure to get everything wrong,' Ransome grumbled. 'Good mind to do them myself,' and he wandered off without another word.

The preliminary sketches were made in three notebooks, one of which he took to Aleppo and contains drawings of camels and Evgenia reading, as well as coloured pencil sketches of Crab Island, Messina Harbour in Turkey and the Kyrenia castle in Cyprus made on their return voyage.

Ransome's bold sketch of his 'hollywood' photograph of Joan and Peggy Hudson that formed the basis of the illustration 'Sums' in *Peter Duck*.

Help came from an unexpected quarter. Colonel Kelsall rigged up a pair of makeshift bunks and fashioned a fine capstan out of a barrel. Desmond, Dick and Joan and Peggy Hudson, posed for photographs, hauling 'halyards', manning the 'capstan' and sitting round a 'camp fire'. A long wooden ladder leaning against the barn wall made splendid shrouds for the children to climb. These 'hollywoods' formed the basis for several illustrations and tailpieces, although Ransome was secretly ashamed of having copied photographs.

The sketches were usually made full size with a soft pencil. There is none of the inhibition of the carefully inked finished pictures and the exploratory sketches have a looseness, freedom and sensitivity of their own. The final versions were a little larger than the reproductions. First they were drawn in pencil and then carefully inked in using Indian ink, after which the pencil lines were erased. His work frequently has the clarity of a technical drawing and an almost oriental concern with shape and detail. He held that narrative and illustrations should combine to make a unified whole. People should be simple representations within a closely observed setting. It is interesting to note that Mary Tourtell and Alfred Bestall adopted the same approach when drawing Rupert Bear and his chums. Ransome's pictures intentionally tell us next-to-nothing about the Swallows and Amazons. As he told the

A study of hats for *Peter Duck* from Arthur Ransome's sketchbook – possibly the work of Dora Altounyan.

The preliminary
sketch for 'Morning
splashes' in *Peter
Duck*.

publisher of the Canadian editions, 'I very much approve of the avoidance of detail in the faces. That is as it should be, but he must be careful not to make the children of the families the wrong comparative size.' In order to avoid showing the children's faces, Ransome usually allows the reader to view the action over somebody's shoulder. He wrote the following explanation:

*There are savage tribes who think it is unlucky to have their portraits made. My characters belong to these savage tribes, and so it is only fair to them that I should guard them from falling under the evil eye of the author.*

*Nancy, my chief collaborator, heartily agrees with me.*

The pictures were finally finished in the middle of August and until the proofs arrived three weeks later, Ransome was able to indulge in an orgy of fishing and sailing *Swallow*. He admitted that he felt pretty tired out, not because of the work but because he thought the book was a failure. They took part in the last of the summer's 'Allcomers' races on Windermere. It was very windy and wet, and in one squall the mast cracked with a loud bang. *Swallow* finished towards the back of the fleet and her crew became soaked to the skin, but both Ransome and Evgenia thoroughly enjoyed the buffeting.

At the end of August the Altounyans arrived for an extended leave and to be near the children while they settled in, as they had finally decided that the time had come for the children to go to school in England. It was a decision that had been reached only after much heart-searching, particularly by Dora. Taqui was now 16, Susie 13, Titty 12 and Roger 10. The girls were to go to Annisgarth School in Windermere and Roger was entered for Abbotsholme School.

In October Ransome consulted Forest Smith again. He pronounced the ulcers cured and explained that they were caused by excess stomach acid that was the result of anxiety, and since that anxiety was due to the pressure of trying to meet newspapers' deadlines, he must give up journalism entirely. Little did he realise that Cape would want a new Ransome for their big children's Christmas book each year, and that struggling to deliver a good book — complete with illustrations — on time, would cause his patient as much anxiety as ever.

*Peter Duck* was published in the middle of October and the print run was again 2, 000 copies. It was dedicated to 'Mrs Robert Blackett and Mrs E.H.R. Walker by way of an apology for the way their children had left them out of their adventures.' Hugh Walpole's favourable review for *The Observer* not only healed a long-standing feud between the two, but also ensured the book's success.

This portrait of Titty Altounyan by her mother was made about the time that Titty went to school in England at the age of twelve. Dora Altounyan made a gift of the painting to the Ransomes, knowing how fond they had become of her.

*The best children's story of the year is Arthur Ransome's* Peter Duck. *Frankly, I find it very difficult to envisage a boy who will not revel in the book. Of course, there are boys (at least I am told so) who wish to read only about Lenin and the Five Years Plan. There are no children's books for them this Christmas. For all the others,* Peter Duck *is the thing,*

*Many of them have already made friends with* Swallows and Amazons *and* Swallowdale. *They were very good, but* Peter Duck *is better. I knew Arthur Ransome twenty-five years ago, and wondered what would prove to be the proper vehicle for his gay and enterprising imagination. He hurried here and he hurried there. He wrote in*

*beautiful prose about all kinds of things from Russia to fishing, but they were none of them exactly his thing. Then, a year or two ago he wrote* Swallows and Amazons, *and after reading the first chapter, I knew we had the best writer for boys in England alive today. Boys of all ages, of course.* Peter Duck *is enchanting. It is so well written that you don't realise that it is written at all. The adventures seem to occur to oneself. If you care for boats, this book is your book, and if you don't care for boats it is also your book.*

*It is long, and there is not a dull page. This is the book for Christmas.*

Then came the news that the Junior Literary Guild had chosen *Peter Duck* for its members — the third Ransome in a row, and the first time anybody had scored a 'hat-trick'! Writing from the Guild, Helen Ferris was already looking towards the next book;

*So go to it, Arthur Ransome, and for your next boys' and girls' book, why don't you do something entirely different with a new set of youngsters? That is not* Swallows and Amazons *by name, so to speak. I think it would be a very good idea, both from the business point of view and from the sheer fun you would have tackling new material. How about it?*

*But whatever you do, good luck.*

Perhaps less welcome was Wren Howard's belief that he should continue to illustrate his books. Ransome freely admitted his difficulty with arms and legs, and would have liked a few lessons on figure drawing had such a thing been possible from such an isolated spot as Low Ludderburn. This did not bother Howard, who remarked that if people laughed, so much the better. Ransome, of course took an entirely different view.

Copies of *Peter Duck* flew off the bookshelves that Christmas and Ransome was positively elated to get a telegram to say that the book was already being reprinted. Freed at last from financial worries, he was able to ponder over Helen Ferris's suggestion about his next book.

# Chapter Six

# WINTER HOLIDAY

IN 1895 WINDERMERE FROZE from end to end and remained frozen for several weeks. Arthur, then aged eleven, had the good fortune to be at his prep school in Windermere at that time and. since the headmaster was an enthusiastic skater, lesson-time was cut short and the boys were able to spend a good deal of time on the ice. These hours were a blessed release from his unhappiness in school, for he was already a fair skater. In the *Autobiography* he tells of whole days spent on the ice, leaving only at dusk as fires and torches were lit and their elders with their lanterns 'shot about like fireflies'. Then in 1929 the lake froze again for a short time,

and Evgenia and he had skated from one side to the other. These memories gave Ransome the inspiration for his new book, and since the lake country was associated so closely with his Swallows and Amazons, there could be no question of taking the advice of Helen Ferris.

The year 1933 opened with the Ransomes' annual climb to the top of the fell behind the cottage in order to hear the New Year being welcomed by a peal of bells from the church across the valley. In the middle of the month Ransome typed a synopsis of *Winter Holiday*. By means of his working notes it is possible to follow some of his creative process in the construction of one of his best-loved books.

It is the last week of the Christmas holidays. The Swallows are staying with the Amazons at Beckfoot while their mother takes advantage of the offer of a buckshee trip to Malta to take Bridget to see her father. Two days before they are due to set off for school, Nancy develops mumps. The doctor insists that the others be isolated for 29 days (Ransome was careful to find out the exact period with his local nurse) and whisks Peggy and the Swallows

**In the winter of 1929 Windermere froze briefly from end to end, and for a few days it was possible to recapture the delights of the Great Frost of 1895. Arthur Ransome took his camera on to the ice to capture this photograph.**

round to Dixon's Farm. The weather has been wet and windy, but there is talk of snow and meanwhile there is a fox hunt to enjoy. Then one morning Titty wakes up to see a bright light on her bedroom ceiling and looks out to see the snow outside. The lake begins to freeze and Mr Dixon takes five pairs of boots to the blacksmith to be fitted with skates. They visit Wild Cat Island and make plans for the Arctic expeditions. Once the lake is frozen sufficiently for John, Susan and Peggy to cross to the other side, they visit Nancy at Beckfoot where the doctor inspects them. There are mentions here of fur hats and a cragfast sheep.

Once the houseboat becomes frozen in, Peggy gets hold of the key and she, John and Susan spend the night in the houseboat that has become Nansen's *Fram*. Here the planning becomes less certain. The single word, 'blizzard' conjures up all sorts of possibilities and there is a suggestion that the Arctic Explorers' base camp be transferred to the Beckfoot boathouse. There is the idea that they might signal to Nancy. Should they race home to Dixon's via Rio and road because of the dark or should they travel over the ice by moonlight? Then there was the notion of making a sail for the toboggan ...

A week later he wrote his first two pages of narrative and changed the nature of the book completely. Elizabeth is talking to herself as Chapter Four begins,

*'They strode on into the freezing night.'*
*'It isn't freezing,' said Dick. 'It must be three or four degrees above freezing point. I wish I hadn't left the thermometer hanging up at home.'*
*'It's graveyard cold anyway,' said Elizabeth.*

In four lines Ransome had established two new characters; the precise, scientifically minded Dick and his romantic gentle elder sister Elizabeth — soon to have her name changed to Dorothea. Why Ransome chose to introduce the newcomers has never been explained. Perhaps it was the attraction of Helen Ferris's suggestion that he write about a new set of youngsters. In that case we have real cause to be grateful. Whether or not he had begun to tire of the Swallows and Amazons, the creation of this delightful couple gave the book its energy and a view both of his Swallows and Amazons and the lake country during a hard winter. Hugh Brogan suggests that Dick and Dorothea are

projections of the two sides of Ransome's character: the young Rugbeian immersed in the activity or interest of the moment and the emerging writer who already has begun to acquire a feeling for language.

At the end of January the Ransomes collected Taqui, Susie and Titty from their school in Windermere and took them to Tarn Hows for skating. Taqui and Susie were able to get along pretty fast, but Titty kicked herself along with one leg — a means of travelling that found its way into the book. That winter the girls often spent the weekend with the Ransomes, and in the barn they listened to the latest chapters until he was quite exhausted. Susie told me, 'On fine days we'd go fishing or sailing. . . Uncle Arthur was very changeable, bubbling over with mirthful laughter if all went well, or growling and cursing if someone displeased him in any way. Aunt Genia had a warm deep voice. . . They could be such fun!'

Several pages of notes written in Ransome's tiny personal hand show how the story was developing. On one page of notes it seems that he was so taken with his new characters that he was content to let the story develop slowly so that the D's do not actually meet with the Polar Explorers until chapter five. The pace of the ending is also slower, occupying eight chapters rather than the six in the book, with the D's trapped at the Pole for longer before the rescuers arrive, followed by the journey homeward. The story ends with the children's return to school. At this stage it was planned that Peggy should arrange the signal that Nancy was out of quarantine. Finally, the possibility that Captain Flint might return was an afterthought — a splendid afterthought that gave Ransome the chance to insert two delightfully humorous episodes.

Sustaining interest through a narrative that covered about five weeks was a considerable challenge. The action in *Swallows and Amazons* and *Swallowdale* had taken place over about a fortnight. It is a testimony to Ransome's skill as a storyteller that he never flags and the book thrusts forward. Ransome drew himself a timeline on which to plot the episodes in the story, moving them around like chess pieces. He fixed on January 18th for the date on which term should begin and January 11th for the arrival of the D's. The party at Beckfoot would take place on January 16th. He decided that the pumpkin holiday should end on February 18th with a return to school. Later this was changed to a more realistic return around February 13th giving February 10th as the date of the D's dash to the Pole.

The final timetable indicates just how well Ransome plotted the long holiday.

| | Date | Pumpkin holiday |
|---|---|---|
| D's travel north | Jan 11 | |
| Signalling to Mars | Jan 12 | |
| Strangers no more | Jan 13 | |
| Skating and the alphabet | Jan 14 | |
| Snow | Jan 15 | |
| Nancy's mumps | Jan 17 | 1 |
| | Jan 18 | 2 |
| Doing without Nancy | Jan 19 | 3 |
| | Jan 20 | 4 |
| Visit to Beckfoot | Jan 21 | 5 |
| Cragfast sheep | Jan 22 | 6 |
| To Spitzbergan by ice | Jan 23 | 7 |
| Nancy gets dispatch | Jan 24 | 8 |
| Nancy sends the key | Jan 25 | 9 |
| First day in the *Fram* | Jan 26 | 10 |
| | Jan 27 | 11 |
| Cache Island | Jan 28 | 12 |
| | Jan 29 | 13 |
| Sailing sledge | Jan 30 | 14 |
| Shove your port legs down — hard | Jan 31 | 15 |
| Dick plans his sail | Feb 1 | 16 |
| Who is sleeping in the *Fram*? | Feb 2 | 17 |
| Captain Flint returns | Feb 3 | 18 |
| Captain Flint visits Nancy | Feb 4 | 19 |
| Captain Flint visits the Pole | Feb 5 | 20 |
| | Feb 6 | 21 |
| Captain Flint, chimney sweep | Feb 7 | 22 |
| | Feb 8 | 23 |
| Dick builds his mast | Feb 9 | 24 |
| Nancy free. The D's sail to the Pole | Feb 10 | 25 |
| (Planned journey north) | Feb 11 | 26 |

On another page Ransome provides an answer to the origin of the North Pole, something that enthusiasts have wrangled good-naturedly for years; writing '(Captain Flint) prepares the "Pole" in a bathing hut at the head of the lake.' I have written elsewhere of the probable locations of the various elements that make up Ransome's lake country, but it seemed worthwhile to follow up this lead. There was a public bathing hut near the mouth of the Rothay-Brathay river for many years. It was a long rectangular building on the shore with its own jetty and is marked on Ordnance Survey maps. There was another bathing hut belonging to the MacIver family who lived at Wanlass Howe, the large house high above the road that runs round the head of the lake, until 1940. Quite by chance, I met Charmian Piper while I was preparing this book. Her grandmother was MacIver's second wife, and while she was growing up in the nineteen twenties and thirties Mrs Piper visited her grandmother regularly. Their portable bathing hut was converted from half the cabin of their 42 ft paddle steamer *Dodo* when it was broken up in 1920. The hut can just be made out on the lakeshore at the eastern end of Borrans Field in some photographs of the period. She confirmed that there was no building in Borrans Park itself — only the two bathing huts. Being a lifelong Ransome enthusiast, her evidence is pretty conclusive. There seems no doubt that one of the bathing huts on the shore was the inspiration for the North Pole, although the building looks as if it owes something to the wooden turret at Brantwood.

The book progressed by fits and starts until February 19th when he completed 59 pages in a continuous run of nine days. On the fourth day he was 'listening' to snatches of dialogue and not concentrating on where he was putting his feet when he fell and broke his ankle. In an unpublished part of his *Autobiography*, he tells the story,

*I had had a good morning's work, and after lunch was walking gaily down the steep hill into the valley when something Roger said so delighted me that, exulting, I whirled my walking stick and came to myself some*

A scene similar to the one that greeted Dick and Dorothea on their first morning on the island with its wintry trees and the snow-covered distant mountains.

*minutes later lying on my back with my head downhill. . .*

Ransome took to his bed at once, and at first they believed that his ankle was not broken, but the next day it was blue and swollen, although there was nothing that could be done immediately as the roads were impassable following a fresh snowfall. As soon as he could reach them, the local doctor examined the ankle and pronounced it broken. There was no telephone at Low Ludderburn, and it was at times like this that the signalling device between the Ransomes and the Kelsalls was invaluable. A simplified version of the code found its way into *Winter Holiday*, for the

Colonel had devised 74 possible combinations of a black wooden square, triangle and cross that were hung on the whitewashed gable end of the cottage, the most frequently used being a square on its own which meant, 'Shall we go fishing?' Across the valley at Barkbooth the Kelsalls hoisted their white-painted signals on the next-door barn.

It is hardly surprising that once confined to his bed, Ransome took stock. He told Wren Howard that the book so far was a complete morass and he feared that he must abandon everything that he had written and start afresh. Given the right scaffolding, he was confident that *Winter Holiday* would make a good book, but he warned Howard that it would take time and he feared another scramble to get it done in time for Christmas.

A couple of days later he told Howard that he was very uncertain if he could provide the illustrations. In his diary he wrote, 'There is something fundamentally wrong with this story. I doubt if Dorothea and Dick fit this strange tale.'

*Winter Holiday* does not reveal the original purpose of the igloo that features in its narrative. It is thought to have been an old charcoal burner's hut but there were other stone structures among the woodlands; Arthur Ransome's illustration shows that the building is not circular and it could have been a bark-peeler's hut. This ruin in Machell Coppice, not far from Peel Island, is a good example of all that remains today.

Heather Beal and Jack Young in Arthur Ransome's workroom at Low Ludderburn recreating his signals to Barkbooth for the BBC Radio Four series, 'On the Trail of Swallows and Amazons'.

The creation of the young Callums had been very satisfying, as Ransome told his mother, 'One at least of the two new characters you won't be able to help liking. I find her a most entertaining companion, and in fact I more than half owe my broken ankle to listening to her conversation, instead of watching my feet.'

By the middle of March, he was firmly stuck and in a stew. A letter written at that time from Dr Forest Smith shows how well he understood his patient.

*I am very sorry that you are having a relapse. I am sure that the whole thing is a vicious circle. Worry and working against time makes the acidity return, this interferes with work and so it goes on. I do not imagine that you have any return of the ulcer.*

*There is no modification to the diet that I can suggest. You seem to be taking those foods which do not stimulate acid formation and of course you are taking appropriate doses of your powder.*

*So sorry to hear about the ankle — that certainly does not help.*

*I enclose a fresh sedative mixture which might help the general condition. Getting the book finished will do still more good.*

*Why do patients with your temperament get these troubles — the people who don't use their brains are much easier to treat!!*

After a month in bed and with the prospect of a further fortnight before he could attempt to put his foot to the ground, Ransome began to fret about the pictures. His problem lay with finding the best way to depict the snowy scene, and he came up with the notion of having grey or brown tinted paper so that he could use white paint as well as black ink. His proposal did not find favour with Cape, for somebody wrote on his letter, 'No. Lots of extra expense and our margin is too thin already.' Instead Wren Howard urged plenty of strong black drawing. Ransome replied, 'I will bear in mind what you say about covering as much ground as possible with black ink so that aunts and such feel that they are getting value for money.'

A fortnight later Ransome told Wren Howard that he was getting more and more disturbed about the pictures and wondered how much it would cost to bring Helene Carter over from America. Even though he had only completed 186 pages of the first draft by the middle of April, he felt he must start the revision, so as to be ready for the holiday on the Broads that they had booked in January. They both greatly needed a break and although he would pay the price later in the summer, Ransome decided to give the book a rest during the month of May. Three weeks were spent sailing, followed by a week in London, looking up old friends.

Ransome worked solidly throughout June and July while the book grew and grew until he had 429 pages that he pruned until it had been reduced to 360 pages of typescript, which he felt was as short as he could make the book. When Cape's secretary wrote asking for a descriptive paragraph that could be used to publicise the book, Ransome replied, 'Bilge!' More than a month later he roused himself to produce a more suitable 'false, lying and optimistic blurb'. On July 24th he wrote to Wren Howard that he was still having a frightful struggle to pull the whole thing into shape and wondering if he should send the manuscript directly to Gray's the printers. The pictures would have to wait until the manuscript was out of the way. 'NB Next year I am going to get my book done and out of the house by May. I'd have done [it] earlier this year but for being laid up.'

He read chapters XXI and XX to Evgenia. She thought that the end of XXII (Next morning) fell flat and XX (Captain Nancy gets two bits of news) immensely repetitive. Ransome agreed, and began to doubt if he could possibly get the book right in time.

A week later Howard received another letter hinting at a slightly more positive frame of mind, 'But "Giminy!" as Nancy would say, it is the very dickens of a job to get some starch into this dishcloth.'

The trouble was that Ransome had been working too intensely, day after day, to the exclusion of any sailing or fishing, while his ulcer got worse and worse. For her part, Evgenia shared his frustration but could do nothing to help except offer her opinion, which she did with complete honesty but with little or no regard for the effect such trenchant criticism would have. She was tired and irritable and needed a complete break, both from Ransome's troubles and the garden in which she had been working much too hard.

Ransome also needed a break from *Winter Holiday* so that he could return afresh before

Captain Nancy
reaching the Pole
by Helene Carter.

making changes but with Cape becoming more and more pressing, that was impossible, and he went ahead as fast as he was able and completed the first revision on August 9th. He spent the following week on revision and posted the first half of the book on August 17th. The printers received the rest of the book without illustrations a week later.

The typescript might have been off his hands but Ransome was still brooding over it when he turned his attention to the full page pictures for the book when he wrote to Wren Howard, 'I can't see what's wrong, and yet I know that something is. So do, for goodness sake have a look at the proofs when they come along.'

The pictures proved to be more time-consuming than he had anticipated. Having worked all morning on the narrative, Ransome found that a couple of sketches were all he could manage that day. Drawing the finished pictures and then inking in usually took two days. One of his sketches is entitled 'Molly [Mrs Blackett] through the snow' and is very like the finished picture 'Nancy reaching the pole'. It seems that at one stage Ransome planned that Molly Blackett as well as her daughter, should set out alone over the ice to rescue the D's.

He confided in Wren Howard, 'John is my trouble. In two of my best drawings he has turned into a clumsy lout of seventeen or eighteen. I can't keep him young. So the only thing to do is to superimpose a younger one on top of him. If I try to do the drawing again I shall spoil it besides wasting time.'

The small decorative tailpieces created problems in spite of their small size and Ransome pleaded with his artistic family and friends for something suitable that he might copy.

He asked Barbara Collingwood, now married to Oscar Gnosspelius and living locally, to draw him a kettle (that was not used until *Coot Club*) and various other things. The medicine bottle and hurricane lantern are probably her work inked in by Ransome. The sailing sledge and Nanson's *Fram* presented less difficulty, and he copied a sheep and a bit of icy road from two of his mother's drawings.

It was not until a week into September that Wren Howard received the proofs. He liked the book and said so. That alone was enough to cheer Ransome immensely, but he also offered some editorial advice — the first time that he had had such an opportunity. He queried the quarantine period for mumps and the precautions taken to ensure that mumps was not transmitted to the others. Ransome checked with the local doctor who confirmed what the nurse had told him and said that the precautions taken in the book were precisely what he himself would advise. Wren Howard also questioned the sweeping effect of the blizzard so that the lake was clear of ice by the time the relief expeditions set out, so that they were able to skate all the way. Ransome agreed to put in a sentence about the 'tremendousness' of the wind. 'I could make them trudge the whole way up the lake, but that would mean that poor Nancy would have to do the same. But I am most anxious to

make it proof against the doubts of children who know ten times as much about ice and skating as I do.'

Then it was discovered that a page that was already at the printers contained an error, and Ransome offered to pay for a new block to be made showing the correct semaphore alphabet. In mid September he sent the remainder, telling Howard to throw out any or all of them but Wren Howard did nothing of the sort. Ransome responded to the news:

*'Hi! I counted on you to hurl forth the worst of those pictures. There are four more full pages than Gray's are expecting. What about that niggly one of them being capsized in the snowstorm, with Dick's legs sticking up as he goes headfirst into the snow. My wife says that picture is a disgrace and I ought not even to have let you see it. I only let it go because I had nowt better, and because a small girl liked it.*

Ruth Atkinson who looked after Cape's publicity designed a neat panel on the jacket to take 'illustrated by the author', but after Ransome's insistence that he did not want it, the wording was changed to 'with many illustrations'. The eye-catching orange jacket was Ransome's suggestion but Cape refused his wish to credit the illustrations to Nancy Blackett on the title page.

Ransome told Wren Howard that the pictures were awful but that he was beginning at last to like some bits of the book. He was not finished with the book that had caused him so much pain for another week or so. Two days later he wrote a comprehensive answer to Wren Howard's suggestion that Mrs Blackett was an unnecessary addition to the gathering for the final scene at the North Pole. After pointing out that he needed the hint of a grown-up view of the escapade, that mothers would think it strange if she were to spend the night asleep in her bed, that children would remember Mrs Blackett dashing off to Wild Cat Island after the stormy night and that she was needed so that the whole secret plan could be explained to her, he went on:

*I cut a dozen pages from that last chapter, in which I took the story right on with Mrs B going back to Dixon's Farm with the Callums, and ending* with their all going back to school together. But that was much worse, and I'm quite sure that the very short ending is much better.

Before *Winter Holiday* was published, Ransome was seized with appendicitis whilst taking a fishing holiday with friends on the Norfolk Broads. After a spell in Norwich Hospital, he convalesced at the King's Head at Wroxham, where he was able to sit in an armchair and fish from the hotel's lawn. Whilst he was there he received visits from several of his friends. Margaret Renold showered him with detective stories, the Kelsalls drove down from Windermere and best of all, Wren Howard arrived with an early copy of *Winter Holiday* bringing with him Molly Hamilton and the news that Cape wanted him to start another as soon as he could. In the middle of November they settled into the Watch House on the waterfront at St Mawes where he spent a further two months recuperating.

When he was well enough to think of books he still had serious concerns about *Winter Holiday's* reception, 'But I think those awful pictures will damn it, even if people don't get bored by the slow start. Still a really gaudy wrapper, with pictures very small, may do the trick for the unlucky buyer.'

*Winter Holiday* was published on November 13th 1933 . It was dedicated to the McEoch family of Cambridge, Massachusetts whose fan letter had apparently made a big impression with their tales of savagery. The number of copies of Winter Holiday printed rose from the 2 000 of *Swallows and Amazons, Swallowdale* and *Peter Duck* to 5 000 — and it was reprinted the following month! He wrote joyfully to give the news to his mother that 1,500 copies were sold the first day — as many *Swallowdale* had sold in a year and more than *Swallows and Amazons*.

Writing in the *New York Herald Tribune* to greet the American edition Mary Lamberton-Becker made some perceptive observations:

*The wonder is that these* Swallows and Amazons *books not only keep up so well but* manage to convince their public that they get steadily better. There was first the brilliant entrance of the two sail-boats and their crews in Swallows and Amazons, *when these groups of children were permitted to spend in the English lake country the sort of summer children most want and least often get — a season devoted to self-organised, serious play, completely unsupervised but sympathetically supported. The adventures of Captain John, Mate Susan, Ableseaman Titty and Ship's Boy Roger (who swims with one foot on the bottom) carried on into* Swallowdale, *the story of a secret valley.*

*In* Peter Duck *they took to blue water in a real ship, combining the best features of* Treasure Island *and* The Bastables. *The three books fitted into the time of year when children really live and grow — the endless freedom of the summer vacation. Now, at an unexpected season, comes* Winter Holiday *to fill the brief period breaking the school year at Christmas time. Nancy's involuntary thoughtfulness in getting mumps ensures a full month for everybody; young readers on both sides of the Atlantic will be grateful to her.*

*These readers will have a sharp shock on the first page; happily it will be brief. There is not a sign of Swallows or Amazons. Instead, in the familiar countryside, now under snow, we meet two children nobody heard of before: Dick and Dorothea. . . I believe that if these books about Swallows and Amazons live — and I cannot imagine their not living a long time — it will be because they lay hold on the underlying continuity of imaginative play, the heartfelt constructive make-believe that carries children along from one generation to another as a cable used once to carry along a car.*

That winter Ransome was not planning a sequel. It seems very likely that he thought that he had finished with the Swallows and Amazons, and that a change of scene to the Norfolk Broads would bring an entirely new cast.

# Chapter Seven

# COOT CLUB

ONCE THEY WERE ESTABLISHED at St Mawes and Ransome was boasting that he could now walk five miles a day 'with considerable *élan*', he began to think about his next book. He had already decided that it would be set on the Broads. He had fished on the Broads briefly in 1914 and again with Ernest Altounyan in 1923. The possibility had occurred to him while sailing the previous spring. In spite of having a foot that had swollen up like a balloon during the day — an after-effect of his broken ankle — Ransome managed to handle their yacht without difficulty. The *Fairway* yachts were the very latest 3-berth sailing cruisers and the summer of 1933 was their first season. Both the Ransomes liked to visit the Broads just after Easter, before most of the motor cruisers had started the season and it was the best time for the bird life. They watched bearded tits and reed warblers among the reed beds, marsh harriers over Hickling and occasionally caught a glimpse of bitterns flying low over the reeds.

Ransome kept a detailed log of the three-week cruise, and it is interesting to spot the episodes that would find their way into *Coot Club*. As well as visiting Roy's of Wroxham, tying up at Horning Hall Farm and watching racing boats go by, towing through bridges, mooring beside a Thames barge at Beccles and watching a fisherman catching eels with a bab, there are numerous details that combine to make *Coot Club* a valuable account of the social and natural history of the Broads as they were more than 70 years ago.

The first week of their cruise was spent sailing around the northern rivers, more or less in company with the Kelsalls who had hired the yacht *Welcome*. The signal-happy Kelsalls were in their element, and on one occasion when they had signalled 'voluntary stop' by flying the 'M' flag in the International Code, the Ransomes failed to understand the signal — much to their acute embarrassment. The second week was spent among the tidal waters of the southern rivers, before they took a tow through Yarmouth and returned to the gentle rivers above Acle Bridge for the last part of their 180-mile cruise.

By the beginning of December, he had the glimmering of an idea. *Coot Club* tells how the D's on a visit to the Broads the following Easter holidays, become caught up in a quarrel between local bird protecting youngsters and a visiting crew of Hullabaloos aboard a motor cruiser, after one of them has cast the cruiser adrift in order to save the chicks of a nesting coot. They become fugitives and are chased all over the Broads before finally being sighted a few moments before the cruiser rams a post on Breydon Water and the hunted turn salvagers.

By means of letters and his notes it is almost possible to 'overhear' Ransome as he develops the story from its unlikely beginning. In his first note the central characters were to be two children whose aunt is unable to cope with looking after them after their parents have gone abroad. A Mrs Towers takes the children and their pug dog off the aunt's hands and away to the country. Here they run across a couple of wild local children whose father, an impoverished artist, is too poor to send them away to school but is teaching them at home (as the Collingwoods had done). The children may behave like savages, but they come from a cultured background. Among the notes there is a vague outline of a scene about a boy in a canoe who approaches the houseboat or yacht of someone that he knows. The boy takes a mudweight from the yacht and sinks his canoe so that he can disappear into the reeds to hide from a pursuing motor boat. When the motor boat turns up, the boat's owner turns accomplice.

In early December he was bemoaning his inability to produce a plot, and appealing to his friend Margaret Renold for help. They had met through Ted Scott in Manchester where her husband, Charles, was Chairman of the Renold Chains and Gears Company, and as enthusiastic about fishing as Ransome. He wrote, 'She was that very rare being in whom authors find it very hard to believe. She was a reader who never wanted to write a book, and one who, if she liked a book, used

'Tom comes sailing home' by Helene Carter.

Several wherry yachts have survived on the Broads serving as a reminder of their Edwardian heyday.

The *Albion* approaching the bend of the river above The Swan at Horning. The *Albion* is not identical to *Sir Garnet*, being the only wherry that was carvel rather than clinker built.

instantly to go to a bookshop and send copies to all her friends.'

He confided that the main character was a local boy, aged about 12, who probably lived in the village of Horning. Then there was a pair of twins who crew their father's racing dinghy. Next there was a lively old lady, a widow and water-colour painter, living in a boat. In the background there are half a dozen local lads. By way of contrast to the old lady, there were two prim and proper girls. He thought that the rivers, stretches of open water and narrow dykes would be a lovely place for his five youthful characters and the old lady. The old lady is impressed by the Principle Boy and contrasts the local youngsters with her well-brought up great nieces or nephews, and invites them for the summer holiday in order that they may develop a 'livelier spirit'.

The Old Lady and the others sail for Norwich leaving the Twins behind so that there can be an exciting chase, as the pursuing Twins hitch lifts on boat after boat. 'What can be devised by way of triumph,' Ransome asked Margaret Renold, 'to be achieved by effort and so provide the happy ending that must almost to the end look as if it can't come off?'

For a time he thought of bringing in Peter Duck, Bill and Peter Duck's wherry *The Arrow of Norwich* to form a link with the other books, but these were too firmly rooted in the romantic imagination of the Swallows and Amazons to fit this realistic tale. Of one thing he was certain. The Swallows and Amazons and Captain Flint were barred! The plot had to make use of the many kinds of Broadland craft and at the same time bring about the sort of stresses between characters that caused the changes of relationship in *Swallows and the Amazons* between the Swallows and the Amazons, the Swallows and Captain Flint, etc.

After a month of trying different ideas, he settled on 'Webfooted Grandmother'. The relationship between the grandmother and her two were to be precisely the opposite of that between the GA and the Amazons. She regards the town children as too desperately proper, and is doing her best to introduce them to the less civilised life of Tom, Port and Starboard and the pirates.

One of the threads of the story is this gradual conversion of the propers, ending with their departure when they are pulling on their gloves and see the faces of Port and Starboard and hurriedly take them off. Evgenia apparently suggested bringing in Dick and Dorothea at an early stage but for a long time he remained undecided.

The middle portion of the book was to be concerned with the conversion of the prim and propers. The boy proper (or Dick) goes overboard while quanting, as part of their education, and Tom makes the boy hang with an arm over the stern while the others quant on. There also has to be some action in which the youngsters act without the old lady. For example, Tom takes the *Titmouse* to Wroxham for stores and errands for Mrs B. The pirates or Port and Starboard overhear the Hullabaloos of the cruiser making enquiries at Horning, so they dash off up the river in their rowing boat and just in time meet Tom and get him to lower the sail of the *Titmouse* and lie in the bottom of the boat beneath it. They tow *Titmouse* down river and home, meeting the cruiser which passes *Titmouse* within a few yards.

On January 22nd 1934 he began. He started setting the scene with Tom, the Bird Protection Society and No 7 nest, followed by the meeting with Mrs Barrable. At this point he got stuck, and apart from taking 16 photographs of William, the Renold's pug to aid his drawing, it was a month before he took the story further. He still does not seem to have fastened on a plot when he wote, 'Tom at Wroxham', 'Aground on Breydon', 'Coots in Council', and 'William on Breydon'. On March 3rd his diary entry reads, '55 pages of bilge', and 'no clue to story yet'. He pressed on and by the end of the month he had completed 113 pages. At the beginning of March he decided to bring in Dick and Dorothea instead of the propers and at last he was able to write a detailed synopsis. The synopsis opens with Tom, having been up river to Colteshall to collect some screws from a boatbuilding friend, sailing past Wroxham greeting his friends along the waterside and checking on nests down the river, past Horning until he reaches the windmill where he lives with his father (a painter or poet). The synopsis then follows the familiar storyline with Tom fitting cupboards, a Coot Club meeting in the shed and the pirates' news of the motor cruiser moored over No 7 nest. When Tom takes refuge beside her houseboat, Mrs Barrable takes the opportunity of asking Tom if he will help her sail a small yacht if she hires one, as she is tired of being in a boat that never moves. Tom is interested but must ask the other Coots. On the strength of this, Mrs Barrable writes to Mrs Callum inviting Dick and Dorothea. She is adopted by the Coots, and for some reason it is the Pirates who meet Dick and Dot off the train as there is some misunderstanding about where they are to meet Mrs Barrable.

A few days later they are all sailing up the River Ant. A visiting yacht is dismasted by Ludham Bridge and salved by the Pirates. Should they continue to Stalham or go through Potter Heigham bridges to Hickling? Should Dick go overboard? And all the time Mrs Barrable is hankering after sailing to the Southern Broads.

Once Book Two *Southern Waters* is reached the synopsis follows the final version quite closely, though Port and Starboard have a mother (rather than a housekeeper) who is worried when she receives the postcard from people that they are supposed to be with.

Towards the end of the synopsis Ransome inserts this aside: 'I think the same motor cruiser with crowd of Hullabaloos should wander in and out from chapter to chapter, so that there is always the danger of Tom being recognised by them. This would give a feeling of outlawry to Tom and in a lesser degree the three Pirates.'

In the middle of April they hired the *Fairway* again and spent three weeks following the eventual course of the *Teasel* to make sure that all the local details were accurate and to take photographs. The cruise also provided first-hand experience of the storm over Oulton in which the *Teasel* arrived at the quay with her deck white with hailstones.

He visited an ornithologist in Norwich who recommended that No 7 should be a coot's nest rather than a water rail's that was difficult to spot from the water. In order to test the feasibility of Tom's journey from Ranworth to Wroxham for stores he took the dinghy from the mooring at Horning Hall (roughly the same distance from Horning as Ranworth) to time the sail to Horning Ferry and back and from that he drew up the following scenario:

*If Tom leaves Ranworth entry at 8, he will be at Wroxham at 11.30. Battery charged 12.30. Nelson's Reach 3.30.*

*D's — 1.30 Leave Ranworth, 2.00 Passed by Margoletta. Row as hard as they can. 2.45 Ferry. 2.50 Get hold of Pete. Bill and Joe away. Pete can't*

*manage the boat. 3.00 P&S are off. Pete bicycles. Think of a way to stop them if you can. D's hang about. 3.30 Pete back from Wroxham. 3.32 Margoletta passes upstream. 3.45 THE MEETING.*

Another example of the care that Ransome was taking in order to have all his details accurate was the letter that he wrote to the owners of the barge *Pudge* that he had seen in Beccles the previous year, asking about the cargoes that they carried and whether their barges used the New Cut or went under the St Olave's Bridge. The company replied that they always used the New Cut when carrying wheat to Beccles and returning with malt or beet from Cantley.

After a few days in London, they were back in Low Ludderburn and from the middle of May until the beginning of September, Ransome was at work on *Coot Club* most days. He fretted over the start which had to make clear that the D's and Mrs Barrable wanted to go sailing but could not do so without Tom's help. Tom's quarrel with the hullabaloos must be seen to have the approval of the D's and Mrs Barrable. Port and Starboard cannot go on the voyage south but must help in the intensive sailing education of the D's.

It was not until July that Ransome decided to bring in the Dick and Dorothea from the beginning so that they meet Tom on the train taking them on the last stage of their journey. This meant completely rewriting chapters I, II and V.

All this work went on against a background of the grief caused by letters from Ivy and Tabitha. Ransome had tried to build bridges with his now adult daughter but the truth of the matter was that they both were carrying too much hurt. Her latest letter, in which she announced that she had married a dock labourer was not believed at first, but when it was confirmed, he was deeply upset.

In the spring they had taken the occasional day off to go and see the progress of the dinghy that was being built by Crossfield's of Arnside for the Renolds. The little boat had been named 'Coch-y-bonddhu' (a Welsh salmon fly) and in early August they snatched another day to take to sail *Cocky* in a race on Windermere, but Evgenia was cold and said *Cocky* was too small. 'But the little boat sailed jolly well!' he noted in his diary.

By this time Evgenia was becoming frustrated with a husband who could think of nothing else except a wretched book that would not come right

Keeping an engineless wherry yacht moving the traditional way is hard work.

The wherry *Maud* lying at the Museum of the Broads was lovingly restored after many years work. Like *Sir Garnet*, *the Maud* was constructed in the traditional way with clinker planking.

Horsey Mere, the wild haunt of bittern and bearded tits, where Dick spotted a Marsh Harrier, is now designated a Site of Special Scientific Interest and a Specially Protected Area for birds.

Close to where Tom Dudgeon's house would have been at Horning is this willow-shaded dyke – just right for the *Titmouse*.

**Arthur Ransome towing his *Fairway* under the railway bridge above Potter Heigham in 1934. (courtesy Brotherton Collection)**

and was falling ill. When at last she was allowed to read the first 14 chapters she found them dull and declared it would never be fit to publish in time for Christmas.

Things came to a head at the beginning of September. Wren Howard wrote saying that he wanted the typescript by the end of the week. 'IMPOSSIBLE', wrote Ransome in his diary. The following day Evgenia told him the figures in his pictures were all wrong and he decided to consult Barbara Gnosspelius. The next day he completed 401 pages of a second draft that he considered needed a new beginning, and somehow or other he would have to cut 50 pages as well.

Two days later Howard revised his deadline to September 7th. At this point, Ransome gave up. Too much needed revising, he told Howard and he was too close to put things right at the moment.

The reaction in Bedford Square was predictable

but a masterly common-sense letter from Howard saved the day. Howard pointed out that he considered that the decision to postpone publication was dangerous for a number of reasons.

*You are all wrong of course — both of you. But as your mind is finally made up we can only accept your decision. It is a dangerous decision as you probably know, but I feel I ought to tell you why I consider it dangerous.*

*The book has already been announced by means of our lists, and advertised in the trade papers in letters to our agents all over the world. Orders have begun to come in as a result of this and the efforts of our travellers. If we now have to say that the book cannot appear until Easter these orders will be cancelled or reduced in size and we shall have* to start all over again. I cannot, I am sure, expect such large orders or such a big total sale in the Spring as in the winter.

Think also of the increasing number of Ransome fans who have been carefully and laboriously coached to expect a book from you each Christmas. They are going to be in the first place disappointed and possibly annoyed and then they are going to buy or have bought for them another instead. Some fortunate ones will be able to afford Coot Club in the Spring but others will either not afford it or will not hear of it.

And do you hope to write another book for publication in the Autumn or to appear always like a Swallow in the Spring, or to miss a year, or what?

When I last saw you I think I said that in my view you were over particular and Mrs Ransome hypercritical. I did not believe then and I don't now that the book is unpublishable even as it is. What you read me was damn good stuff. And I still maintain that it would be far less dangerous to let the book go to the printer now, even if it were not so highly polished as you both wish. My advice therefore is once more, to send off immediately as much of the book as you can to Gray [the printer], and to tinker with the balance for another week when it too should go to Scotland.

IT WILL LOOK MUCH BETTER IN TYPE

But I don't for a moment suppose that you will take this advice, so I have written gloomily to the unfortunate Gray.

Horning Regatta in the 1950s by the Swan Inn. *Flash* and her sisters were Yare and Bure One Designs, known as the White Boats. Racing is just as fierce today as when *Flash* won by the length of her short bowsprit.

Arthur Ransome made this careful sketch of the mizzen mast of the barge *Pudge of Rochester* when they were moored alongside at Beccles in 1933.

**With all its fenders out, a yacht similar to the *Teasel* threads its way beneath the notorious road bridge at Potter Heigham.**

On the day that he received Howard's letter Ransome went back to work and nine days later he sent the typescript to Grays. During the next fortnight he was fully occupied with the illustrations, many of which were based on the photographs he had taken. He covered 73 pages in his sketchbook with drawings from which he produced the necessary 19 full page illustrations.

At the beginning of November he travelled to Edinburgh to go through the proofs in order to save every possible day, and three weeks after that he was handling the advance copies. He would immediately have spotted one of the more obvious effects of the revisions that he made since Howard last had a sight of it. In the publishers blurb on the dust jacket the *Teasel* is called 'Daisy'! Ransome's slip of the pen when he wrote Stalham instead of Salhouse resulted in Cape having to print more than 7,000 erratum slips. 4,000 copies were printed and a further 3,000 later in the month, and by Christmas more than 5,000 had been sold. By this time, Ransome had become a familiar visitor at local booksellers in Kendal, Windermere and Ambleside when he looked in to check on his sales.

Beyond the entrance to Kendal Dyke, the River Thurne is among the
quietest parts of the Broads. This yacht is also similar to the *Teasel*.

The tree-lined River Bure between Ranworth entrance and Horning was the
haunt of the Coot Club, and the scene of their regular patrols during spring.

Sylvia Lynd, who had been one of the young ladies to whom Ransome had lightheartedly proposed marriage, reviewed *Coot Club* for the Book Society Annual.

*Mr Ransome must be one of the few living authors whose books are demanded as a matter of course by children at Christmas. The English will remain a seagoing people, or at any rate a lake and river going people, as long as the young of the race read Mr Ransome. Messing about with water has always been one of mankind's earliest pleasures, and the life of pottering with lovely sails and brave tumblings overboard that we live with Mr Ransome is simply irresistible.*

In 1984 *Coot Club* was dramatized for BBC Television as half (with *The Big Six*) of the strangely named 'Swallows and Amazons For Ever' serial with Rosemary Leach as Mrs Barrable, Harry Dimbleby (the son of the TV presenter) as Tom and three local lads as the Death and Glories.

*Swallows and Amazons* and *Swallowdale* had sprung from his childhood holidays, *Winter Holiday* had its origin in his experiences of the Great Frost of 1895 and *Coot Club* had been closely linked to their Broads cruises but his next book would be a land-based affair arising out of the activities of a friend.

Arthur Ransome's unused sketch for *Coot Club*.

# Chapter Eight

# PIGEON POST

THE YEAR 1935 BEGAN BADLY for Ransome. He drove down to look at sailing boats at Brixham and to have lunch with Ivy in Teignmouth. Ivy told him that Tabitha had tricked her young man into marriage, also that her husband was deformed and half-witted. Even allowing for Ivy's partiality for dramatisation, Ransome was disturbed by her news. Perhaps he was not concentrating when his car skidded off the road near Hereford, turned over on its side and went backwards into a ditch. Ransome got off very lightly with only a bruised head and a cut leg. It is not clear how he managed to extricate the car, but he had to buy a replacement tail lamp in Leominster, before driving to Shrewsbury. The following month he bought a new car.

It is very difficult to trace the development of *Pigeon Post* in any sort of detail. The Cape-Ransome archive in Reading University contains no letters relating to the book's progress and publication, and only a fragment of Ransome's working notes has survived to throw light on the book's progress. It seems likely however, that he followed his usual practice of making a list of chapter headings and then writing chapters in the order that appealed to him, or according to difficulty, leaving the hardest until last and then reworking the beginning.

*Pigeon Post* owes its existence to the mining activities of Barbara Collingwood's husband Oscar Gnosspelius. He had trained as a civil engineer and had spent time in the Transvaal, Angola and Brazil. He became interested in flight in the years before the First World War and designed the Gnosspelius hydro-monoplane that took off from Lake Windermere in 1912. During the war he served with the Royal Naval Air Service. After the war he was with Short Brothers in the test department. The two men had known each other for some years, and in July 1929 Ransome went to tea with them and noted in his diary that Gnosspelius had discovered copper on the slopes of Coniston Old Man.

The mine is situated about 1,600 feet up under the shoulder of Brimfell and is known as 'John 'Willie' Shaw's Level' after the miner who daily trudged up from the village to work. Shaw tunnelled for around 100 yards, before abandoning the working four years later. The vein can clearly be seen above the tunnel mouth, but there was never enough copper ore to make the mine a commercial proposition. After this attempt, Gnosspelius set up 'Willie' Shaw in a small slate mine in the Tilberthwaite Valley. According to Eric Holland in his book *Coniston Copper Mines*, the copper mine in the country above that Ransome renamed High Topps was once linked to the quarry but the journey was not the comparatively easy underground passages of the hurrying moles in *Pigeon Post*, but a matter of descending vertical ladder-shafts for several hundred feet.

The first hint of *Pigeon Post* is the entry in Ransome's diary in the middle of February 1935 when Barbara and Oscar Gnosspelius went to tea at Low Ludderburn and Oscar was very helpful with the mining details.

On February 25th — much later in the year than usual — he wrote the first page and, in the manner of Dorothea, came to a halt. A week later he took the first chapter on for a further four pages with the release of pigeons at Strickland Junction. By the end of March he had only reached 82 pages of rough draft. On March 27th he wrote in his diary, 'Went up behind Tilberthwaite with Gnossie. Saw several of the old workings and a suitable bit of country for my story'.

The following day was spent house-hunting. There had been a half-hearted attempt to leave Low Ludderburn several years earlier, but this time their minds were made up. There were several reasons for this. The rainy Lake District climate did not agree with Evgenia and the poor soil was frustrating to a gardener of her ambition. The success of the Swallows books had provided them with a degree of financial security at last, for in 1934 the royalties alone had taken Ransome into the £1 000-a-year class. They were both still hankering after the halcyon *Racundra* days, and

The Old Man towers over the village of Coniston that was once the home of the numerous miners who for six days a week trudged many hundreds of feet up to their work.

The plateau (High Topps) beneath the peak of Wetherlam is a wild, lonely place, and potentially dangerous because of the mine entrances and shafts.

Until recently little had changed at Rio Bay since Titty and Roger wandered down a landing stage at the beginning of *Pigeon Post* and saw *Amazon* coming to fetch them. The landing stages have now been rebuilt.

there was no doubt that Ransome's health improved when he was afloat.

The huge sales of the *Winter Holiday* and *Coot Club* had made it possible to contemplate both a move and the acquisition of a much larger boat than poor *Swallow*, that had been out of favour since the Renolds had decided that sailing was not for them and presented him with the faster *Coch-y-bonddhu*. Five years earlier he had looked forward to the day when he might become one of those writers who could sell 3 000 copies a year. Sales for *Coot Club* alone had already reached 7,000. It is little wonder they had become unsettled! Ransome's family were alarmed to hear that Evgenia was stipulating that they find a large house and garden with all the modern conveniences and two servants to do the work! Meanwhile, Low Ludderburn was put on the market and Ransome pressed on with *Pigeon Post*. The story opens with the whole cast of eight from

'Mrs Tyson made me look in a mirror' by Mary Shepard.

*Winter Holiday* camped on the Beckfoot lawn, as the Walkers will be without the use of *Swallow* until their mother arrives at Holly Howe with Bridget. This is no handicap, because Nancy is sickened by her uncle dashing off in search of gold instead of joining in her latest ploy, and having heard a rumour that there is gold hidden in the fells nearby, she has set everyone off to hunt for it. They visit an old miner working deep underground who can tell them where to start their search. Slater Bob and his mine was based on 'Willie' Shaw and his underground quarry in the Tilberthwaite Deep Level. As they leave the mine, they are on the point of giving up the idea because the gold is too far from Beckfoot, when they see a stranger about to call on Slater Bob. He is the same strange man they have seen peering over the Beckfoot gate. Nancy decides that he must have overheard them planning, and the man with his squashy hat becomes an unsuspecting rival. In order to find the gold before their rival, they need to camp much nearer to the gold fields, and Mrs Blackett reluctantly allows them to camp in a distant farm orchard on condition that they send a pigeon home each day to let her know that all is well.

Thanks to Titty's discovery that there is water for camping on the edge of the High Topps gold fields they are able to break free of the restricting hospitality of the farmer's wife, and the camp cooks, Susan and Peggy, are able to put Susan's new mincing machine to good use. Having found what they believe to be gold there is much earnest crushing, panning and smelting, whilst others keep watch to see that their rival has no chance to discover their mine.

'Done it after all! … Barbecued Billygoats!' by Mary Shepard.

The younger ones naively stray into a tunnel that proves to be unsafe, and they are all but trapped underground. Later in the book there is even greater danger when the fell catches fire. When Captain Flint returns, he explains that what they have found is a rich vein of copper ore and what is more, their hated rival, the man they have called Squashy Hat is really his partner who had come on ahead and had been unsuccessfully trying to find 'their' copper.

The ingenious contrivance that rings a bell when a pigeon returns with a message, was the invention of twelve years old Dick Kelsall. Using a wooden fruit box and some of his father's wire, bits of brass for contacts and a couple of Leclanché wet cells he was able to show Ransome that the thing actually worked!

Very early in the planning stage Ransome had decided that the story would centre on the four younger ones, and as far as possible tell the tale from their viewpoint. The book opens with the arrival of Titty and Roger from their school. When John, Susan and Nancy are searching for a camping place, the narrative remains with the stay-at-homes at Beckfoot. One of the finest chapters in the entire canon describes Titty's feelings as she overcomes her fear of dowsing in order to discover an underground spring.

'Sitting on the ladder by the pigeon loft' by Mary Shepard.

*Titty swallowed once or twice. No one was here to see. No one would know if, after all she could not bring herself to do it.*

*'Oh, come on,' she said to herself. 'You've got to. Better get it over.'*

*She turned the twig round and took the two ends, one in each hand just as Nancy had shown her by Mrs Tyson's pump. She found herself breathing very fast.*

*'Duffer,' she said firmly. 'You can just drop it if you want'*

The chapter 'Roger Alone' tells how, whilst playing around, he discovers the gold. Two chapters are devoted to Dick, Dorothea, Titty and Roger's adventure underground.

For Ransome, life during the early part of summer revolved around showing Low Ludderburn to potential buyers and pressing on with 'The Grubbers' — as he was calling it. Oscar Gnosspelius, who was translated into print as Squashy Hat, showed Ransome how to pan for

**Colonel Jolys by Mary Shepard.**

Beacon Tarn (Trout Tarn) is one of the loveliest of lowland tarns, seen here against a backdrop of the Coniston fells. The fishing, although controlled, is nearly as good as it was when Captain Flint taught John and Susan to cast a fly.

gold and he took him high up the mountain to Swallow Scar to view the location for the gold fields from above. Ransome enjoyed the experience but suffered a recurrence of his stomach trouble for his pains.

By the end of June the first draft was complete and Ransome confided in his diary, 'Read all through. AWFUL. No grip anywhere. Masses of corroborating detail needed. No tension,' and 'the whole book is somehow not there. No drama . . . and worse.'

The revision occupied Ransome for a week in July and the first week in August and then stopped. It was, he thought, 'all but lifeless' and he complained that he was unable to concentrate on

it. In the event he was unable to pick it up until the following February. Cape would have to accept that there would be no Ransome for Christmas that year. For his part, Ransome agreed that the book would not be called 'The Grubbers', 'Grubbers All' or 'High Topps' but Wren Howard's much preferred and better title, 'Pigeon Post'. In order to justify the change of title Ransome knew that he would need to bring in more about the pigeons and neatly worked in Sappho's call for help when the fell caught fire.

At the end of July they had driven down to Essex and looked around that area between Ipswich and Shotley that Evgenia had chosen, and on August 6th they agreed terms for their new

Horse Crag Quarry (the underground cavern where the prospectors met Slater Bob). (courtesy of Tom Alexander)

Arthur Ransome filled several sketchbooks with drawings for the illustrations. Occasionally he drew on thick water-colour paper, but most of the books had thin paper – almost like tracing paper – with perforations for easy removal.

The entrance to Horse Crag Level (Slater Bob's mine).

home. Broke Farm is situated in the village of Levington and close to the north shore of the River Orwell. Ransome described the place in a draft for his *Autobiography*:

*Broke Farm was originally the home farm of Broke Hall. It was a plain red brick house with cowsheds and dairy on one side of it and on the other a row of cottages. From the upper room in which I worked, I could see the river and the mouth of Levington Creek, with Harwich harbour and in the distance Landguard Point and the open sea.*

The house was not, perhaps, as large as Evgenia would have wished, for she laid down the law that for every new book that Ransome acquired he would have to dispose of one in order that his library would not continue to grow indefinitely. While she supervised the preparations for their departure from Low Ludderburn, Ransome went to Poole to have a look at a cruising yacht that had been recommended to him. He bought her on the spot, after a token show of haggling over the price. This was the much-loved *Nancy Blackett*, and with the help of a strong young man he sailed her around the coast to Pin Mill, just across the river from his new home where they had planned to keep the yacht..

The actual move took place towards the end of October.

According to Ransome's sailing log, *Nancy Blackett's* first visitors were Wren Howard and his wife and son Michael, who drove up from London for the day at the beginning of November and were taken down the river. The following weekend Taqui Altounyan and a friend from school came to sample life aboard, but the weather was beastly and the friend was seasick whilst they were still on the mooring. The story of Ransome's favourite yacht might have been very different had Evgenia not been such an enthusiastic cook, for she took against the *Nancy Blackett* from the start because the cabin, and particularly the galley, was too small.

At first Ransome found much to do aboard, but he did manage to make a start on the new set of illustrations for *Swallows and Amazons* and *Swallowdale* that Cape had been urging him to produce. In the lakes there had been the Kelsall boys and Hudson girls to join in making the 'hollywoods' for *Pigeon Post*, and Gnosspelius's

daughter Janet had posed for a photograph showing how to use a blowpipe on the gold dust but at Levington there was only the noisy child of the next-door neighbour who disturbed Ransome when he wanted to concentrate; 'if that child had fallen out of her window and broken her neck I think I should have regarded it as a dispensation of Providence, and kindly dispensation too'.

For a time, winter maintenance took the place of fishing. Ransome would disappear into the attic where everything that could be removed from *Nancy Blackett* had been stored, to scrape and varnish blocks, grease wire rigging, and paint the lanterns.

After Christmas 1935 Ransome settled to work on the illustrations for *Swallowdale*. In between recording his games of squash, planning *We Didn't Mean to Go to Sea* and bursts of revising *Pigeon Post*, Ransome's diary includes entries such as 'Inked "On the March"' and 'Pencil, "Stop him!"' (the parrot chewing the arrow). *Swallowdale* is the most lavishly illustrated of the series with 28 full-page illustrations, 11 headpieces and 13 tailpieces.

It was well into April before Ransome could bring himself to settle to the *Pigeon Post* revision, having completed the *Swallowdale* illustrations. 'I am written out and done for', he gloomed in his diary. 'There is no other explanation for my complete inability to concentrate.' Two possible explanations spring readily to mind: in spite of the attractions of Levington, Ransome was missing the Lake District and the daily stimulus of the view of the distant hills, and the other was his 7-ton cutter bobbing about at her moorings on the other side of the River Orwell waiting to go to sea.

Ransome's mother paid them a visit that spring and was charmed with the place. From her bed in the spare room she could see steamers criss-crossing on their way to and from Ipswich. The home was comfortable, light and airy, quite unlike the shut-in feeling of Low Ludderburn with its three feet thick walls and small windows. Evgenia had made it quite pretty, and although it was not as large as she had hoped, there was the advantage of a decent garden for her to tend.

It was not until the end of May that Ransome took time off to sail *Nancy Blackett*. The object of the cruise was to test the credibility of the plot of his next book by sailing to Holland. The cruise lasted twelve days in which time Ransome sailed 218 miles from Pin Mill to Flushing and returned via Ostend.

Satisfied that his new plot would work, Ransome spent the next six weeks revising 170 pages of *Pigeon Post*. Having reached a stage where it was ready for Evgenia to read, Ransome sailed away in *Nancy Blackett* to Brightlingsea for the weekend with a friend from his Rugby days, Philip Rouse, and returned fearful of her verdict. In Evgenia's opinion the book was not very much worse than the worst of the others and only three chapters needed further revision!

Eventually he revised 'Consulting Slater Bob', 'Mrs Blackett makes conditions', 'Pioneers and stay-at-homes', 'Prospecting', 'Fending off the enemy', 'Pot of paint' and 'Can't anybody dowse?' On August 22nd he sent the typescript to Wren Howard who was mackeral fishing in the Scilly Isles. It was, he told his mother, much duller than *Peter Duck* and just as long and he warned Howard to look out for any contradictions in the text that he feared had crept in with the rapid revision. A week later a further typescript was on its way to the U.S.A and he was free to 'barge ahead' with the pictures that by then were urgently needed.

He had hoped that Ruth Atkinson, the artistic designer of Cape's unique dust jackets would help by improving the figures, but it is unlikely that such help materialised. He bewailed having to use ink rather than water-colour that was 'hard, unyielding stuff by comparison'. Writing to the schoolgirl author, Pamela Whitlock who was illustrating *The Far-distant Oxus* for publication the following year, he advised 'Indian ink and a fairly thick pen to avoid scratchiness'.

His own illustrations for *Pigeon Post* were preceded by 43 pages of sketches that in some cases convey greater feeling than the finished versions that may have the clarity of a technical drawing but little more. An example is 'The pigeon loft' in which the four figures are drawn well, but nothing of the special character of the Cumbrian stone wall is suggested. It might have been built of breeze blocks.

Ransome's work is a little too precise. The sketches, drawn with a soft and rather thick pencil have a freedom and feeling that the finished versions lack. The delightful little sketch for 'Slater Bob Talks of Gold' has more atmosphere than the inked version that suffers from the limitations that Ransome experienced with pen and ink, whereas Pamela Whitlock seems to have used a brush and two thicknesses of nib to achieve what Ransome

called 'gorgeous lively things to match the spirit of the book'.

Five thousand copies of *Pigeon Post* were printed and two further impressions before publication on November 13th. The book trade and the buying public seemed to agree with Howard Spring's verdict that *Pigeon Post* was, 'Typical Ransome, which is to say that it is in a class that out-tops by head and shoulders, and half a body the customary stuff'.

Once *Pigeon Post* was finished there was time for a little sailing to be had in what remained of the autumn of 1936 before *Nancy Blackett* was put on a mud berth for the winter. He planned to spend more time afloat the following year and when he learned that *Pigeon Post* had been awarded the Carnegie Medal, his first reaction was to say that he would be too busy sailing to receive it in person.

**The prospectors by Mary Shepard.**

There was a reason for this apparent lack of interest, because the award was a new venture by the Library Association to celebrate the centenary of Andrew Carnegie and neither author nor publisher had heard of it. Ransome valued the letter of congratulation signed by the entire staff of Jonathan Cape, but remained sceptical about the award, writing to Wren Howard:

*Has the award (if not a hoax) been announced in the newspapers or is it something that the Library Ass. does, so to speak on the sly? Or do we have to boost the Library Ass. by announcing it ourselves. The whole thing seems to me extremely odd. . . I wonder what the medal's made of?*

Someone at the publishers noted on Ransome's letter that a press release had been given to Reuters and Central News.

He was still feeling doubtful when he wrote to Helen Ferris of the American Junior Literary Guild book club telling her of his 'queer bit of news'. Naturally enough, she took an entirely different view:

Mary's Shepard's tailpiece showing Squashy Hat as spied upon by the scouts in *Pigeon Post*.

*For once the famous Arthur Ransome vocabulary crashes to the ground in failure! 'Queer bit of news' indeed! A gorgeous bit of news, a glorious bit of news!!*

*The boat that brings this letter to you will be deep in the water with its load of congratulations from us — but congratulations, truly, fully as much for the Library Association on their discrimination and intelligence as to Arthur Ransome on the honor that has come to him.*

*So what-ho and greetings and happiness that the new book is under way.*

In spite of his intention to give the presentation ceremony a miss, Ransome collected the prestigious Carnegie Medal for the best childrens' book of 1936 in Scarborough from Archbishop Temple in front of 1 200 people and was, according to his mother, 'dithering with fright'. The lack of publicity annoyed Ransome who grumbled that they might just as well have sent it by post and saved him the journey. He was also aggrieved to find that the medal, although golden coloured was not gold. 'Please don't bite it or try to bend it,' he cautioned Ruth Atkinson when he sent the medal for the Cape staff to admire.

By the time that he received the medal he was already trying to put some life into *We Didn't Mean to Go to Sea* before allowing Evgenia to read it.

Squashy Hat asleep under his map.

'Squashy Hat asleep under his map'. Arthur Ransome's unused sketch for *Pigeon Post*.

# Chapter Nine

# WE DIDN'T MEAN TO GO TO SEA

IN JANUARY 1936, only four months after he had become the Master and Owner of *Nancy Blackett*, Ransome wrote joyfully to Wren Howard:

*During the last four days I have seen, grabbed, clutched and pinioned a really gorgeous idea for another book . . . Swallows only . . . No Nancy or Peggy or Captain Flint . . . But a GORGEOUS idea with a first-class climax inevitable and handed out on a plate . . . lovely new angle of technical approach and everything else I could wish. So I breathe again. I really was afraid that I had done for myself or rather for those stories by uprooting, but I haven't. This new idea is the best since Swallows and Amazons.*

After the complex plot of *Pigeon Post*, the story of *We Didn't Mean to Go to Sea* is probably the simplest of the series. On the day after the fire on High Topps in *Pigeon Post* a telegram arrives to say that Commander Walker is on his way home from the China Station to take up a shore command and his family must go south to meet him instead of having naval battles with Captain Flint and Timothy. They take lodgings at Pin Mill and fall in with a capable young skipper of the *Goblin* — a yacht that is *Nancy Blackett* in everything but name and number. The Swallows are allowed to crew aboard the *Goblin* for a couple of days, so long as they do not go outside Harwich harbour. Next morning the wind fails and they run out of fuel at dead low water near the harbour mouth. The young skipper (perhaps he is not that

capable?) rows ashore in the dinghy in search of petrol. Unbeknown to the children he meets with an accident, and when the *Goblin*'s anchor drags near high water, they find themselves drifting out to sea in a fog. The wind blows the fog away but they discover that turning round and battling into it is all but impossible. There is no alternative but to go on and get well clear of the land. The following morning they find themselves off the coast of Holland. Sensibly taking on board a pilot to guide them into harbour, they are just in time for Commander Walker to jump ship in Flushing and take a passage home in the *Goblin*.

In his book *The Magic of the Swatchways*, Maurice Griffiths tells the story how in 1932 his wife set out from Harwich on the ebb tide to be caught in the fog outside. They heard the 'dismal moan' of the Sunk lightship and as they crossed the North Sea, had a close encounter with a steamer in the dark and steered through patches of floating flotsam — episodes that found their way into *We Didn't Mean to Go to Sea*. However, the book owes a great deal to Ransome's own North Sea crossing in June 1936. He was still just as meticulous over details such as timing that had led him to enact part of Tom Dudgeon's sail from Ranworth to Wroxham in *Coot Club*. He badly needed to know how long it would be before the *Goblin* brought up in Flushing, as well as collecting the local colour that he needed for the foreign port.

Evgenia flatly refused to sail and Ransome was forced to hire a young man who, he discovered too late, had no experience of sailing at sea and spent most of the voyage on his bunk. Ransome duly paid his fare home and was relieved to be rid of him. Whilst he was in port he met E. de Smit, a pilot who would make his appearance in the story. de Smit found a young Dutch seaman that Ransome found 'very pleasant indeed' to crew for the return passage at £1 per day, and they sailed south to Ostend before crossing to Harwich.

So eager to start on the 'seabook' had Ransome been, that for a few days in February he abandoned the pictures for *Swallowdale* and the *Pigeon Post* revision and wrote the first 26 pages.

Once he had received the advance copies of *Pigeon Post* in early November, he wrote 'Fog and Tide', 'The Beach End Buoy', 'Drifting Blind' and 'Woolworth Plate' chapters, encouraged by the news from Cape that 6 000 copies of *Pigeon Post* had been sold well before Christmas. By the New Year he had completed 111 pages of rough draft, drawn five small pictures and had made a start on the endpaper chart. Hopefully, there would be no mad scramble to have the book ready for Christmas 1937!

These were years of steadily increasing royalties. In 1936 the sales of *Swallows and Amazons* had been 1342 copies, *Swallowdale* 890, *Peter Duck* 847, *Winter Holiday* 744, *Coot Club* 764 and Pigeon Post 7934. On the strength of these figures he ordered a new Austin car and collected it from the works the following month.

On January 3rd he braved the elements and sailed *Coch-y-bonddhu* across to Pin Mill and back and was pleased with the way the little boat carried full sail in spite of being buffeted by the harder puffs.

Ransome's mother sent him a copy of the *North Sea Pilot* for his birthday and in writing to thank her he remarked how useful it would be for his new book and let out a few secrets; Jim Brading has just left Rugby, and at that stage he planned to introduce a sailmaker, a greengrocer and a bargee, but there is no mention of Customs Officers.

The first person in the list of characters was Annie Powell of Alma Cottage, just up the lane from the But and Oyster Inn. In order to prepare the way for her inclusion in the book, he presented her with copies of *Swallows and Amazons* and *Winter Holiday*.

By the end of January, Ransome had reached the half-way stage with 160 pages completed and was negotiating with Macmillan to publish future books in America. The Junior Literary Guild had proved to be very good friends and had taken all six of the titles, but he felt that apart from these sales, Lippencott had not expected to sell many copies. The only snag was that Macmillan and the JLG had different views about the 'business end of things'. He parted company with the JLG and Helen Ferris with deep regret and decided to take a chance with Macmillan.

The following month the BBC Children's Hour broadcast an abridged reading of *Peter Duck*. The previous year there had been a dramatised version of *Swallows and Amazons* broadcast in five episodes, but Ransome was relieved to hear that the proposal was for 17 readings each lasting 20 minutes. The production brought together the Children's Hour's classic combination of David Davis who did an adaptation that was read by Derek McCulloch (Uncle Mac). On the strength of the fee of ten guineas for each episode, Ransome

announced that he had ordered a new sextant and would purchase a hand-bearing compass. During the summer, he promised himself, he would have a try for Norway.

Then, completely out of the blue, he received a large fat envelope containing many sheets of manuscript. By this time he was well-accustomed to receiving fan-letters and had a decorated card printed leaving a small space in the middle on which to reply. There had been an amusing one from a girl who had said, 'Please write another book exactly like the last, with the same people, the same places and the same things happening'. Particularly welcome were those from abroad. A girl had written from South Africa to say that she knew that he was writing about her own country because near her home was a lake with all the locations that she had read about. A box of dates arrived from a little girl in California, and an American mother had invited the characters to come over to America to spend their summer holidays with her small son. Several of his young correspondents had told him that they had started to write a book but nobody had sent anything like this.

The manuscript was a full-length book that had been the collaborative effort of two teenage girls, Katherine Hull and Pamela Whitlock, who were aged 14 and 15 when they started. *The Far-Distant Oxus* was a remarkable achievement as they had written in secret at their boarding school in Ascot, and not even their parents knew. On the surface it might have been just another pony book. The story tells of an idyllic summer holiday spent on Exmoor, yet it is the children's imaginative fantasy and the writers' energy and eye for detail that makes the book special. Having finished, they wondered what to do with it, and eventually decided to send it to Ransome in case Titty or Roger might like it.

A day or so after he had read the manuscript, Ransome took it to Cape who readily agreed to publish. The parents were pleased to allow Ransome to act for the children and so he became the book's Godfather. Jonathan Cape warned that the book would be 'passed over' unless Ransome wrote a long introduction. If the book had a good send off, he thought that it would continue to sell. Ransome did as he was asked, and Cape was proved right in his assessment, for more than seventy years after publication *The Far-Distant Oxus* is still in print. English mistresses might have found things with which to cavil but Ransome recognised the special nature of the book, and when Cape's reader suggested that it was necessary to 'revise' certain passages, he fought for the book's integrity, replying that it was 'absolutely essential that we shall be able to say that we are printing the book EXACTLY AS IT CAME FROM THE SCHOOL DORMITORY IN WHICH THE AUTHORS BREAKING ALL RULES PUT IT TOGETHER THEMSELVES'. Wren Howard did not agree with Ransome, but recognised that in matters like that it was useless to argue, and only the spelling errors were corrected.

Throughout the months of April and May, Ransome made virtually no progress with *We Didn't Mean to Go to Sea*. Part of this time was spent getting *Nancy Blackett* ready for sea but he still suffered from bouts of his stomach troubles from time to time. When the yacht was rigged to his liking they went round to the Walton Backwaters and took two young novices aboard for a return passage to Pin Mill. These were George and Josephine Russell from nearby Broke Hall, and Ransome was delighted with the way they stood up to the hard squalls and rain showers that they met outside the harbour. Evgenia had a different view and announced that the yacht was too small for more than two aboard. A day or so later they all went to the circus. Comparing notes afterwards, George and Josephine agreed that although they had each enjoyed the show, Ransome had laughed more than anyone. From then on, whenever they were on holiday, Ransome was able to call on George and Josephine to crew for him.

In May he made one of his most satisfying cruises, taking *Nancy Blackett* down Channel to Portsmouth with Philip Rouse and returning just in time for Rouse to

Arthur Ransome's preliminary sketch for 'Candle-grease Aunt'. Did his mother add the studies of hands and feet while she was staying at Broke Farm?

return to work. Later he wrote the cruise up for the Cruising Association Bulletin under the title 'Saturday to Saturday'.

By the middle of June the draft was ready for Evgenia's inspection. By this time Ransome was long past relishing the technical problems that he had foreseen 18 months earlier, and doubts had come crowding in. 'It's a dreadfully seasick book . . . at the moment it seems a failure', he told Helen Ferris.

Pin Mill, one of the favourite haunts of East Coast yachtsmen, is still very much a working community.

*Nancy Blackett* reaching through the moored yachts in the River Orwell at Pin Mill in 2009.

*We Didn't Mean to Go to Sea* was published on November 12th as Howard had intended, and the original print run of 6,000 had been increased by a further 5,280 by publication day. The anonymous critic in *The New York Herald Tribune* must have gone some way to calming Ransome's fears that it was undesirable for readers to meet the Swallows for the first time in *We Didn't Mean to Go to Sea*.

*Arthur Ransome may go down in history as one author who wrote books for young people in a series that began from the first every time. It is an art. He practices it in various ways. Sometimes the scene changes, sometimes the time of year transforms the scene: often a few favourite characters come in without clogging the stage; sometimes a minor character, staying through other books in the wings, suddenly takes a leading part. However it happens, the result is the same; you can start anywhere. Here, for instance, you find in the first chapter a family of young folks — John, Roger, Susan and Titty — sitting in a borrowed dinghy on the river near Ipswich, and may know no more about them than you at once find out — that they have had plenty of experience in open craft but never the chance to sleep on board a boat with a cabin. That is all you need to know to start fair with any one who began his Ransome with* Swallows and Amazons.

Just three days after posting his last picture to the printers, Ransome was off to Wroxham for their fishing holiday aboard the motor cruiser *Royal Star*. The Broads were deserted at this time except for other fishermen, and on the following three days he competed with Evgenia to see who could catch the most roach, dace and bream. The scores were 16-14, 17-13 and 9-11 in his favour, but Evgenia had the better fish. The pain that Ransome had first felt as he was straining to free a jammed rope aboard *Nancy Blackett* a couple of weeks before, was not improved by jumping ashore and mooring or unmooring the large cruiser, and the surgeon that he consulted told him that an operation for umbilical hernia would make him better than new. He went into a nursing home in Norwich on November 23rd.

Wren Howard had already jogged his elbow with an idea for the next book. 'I have an idea that the next book might perhaps revolve around Roger, presumably Titty and some new characters from Pin Mill. Temporary exclusion of John and Susan would give a new focal point and age level,' but Ransome was not thinking about books. Around his room in the nursing home were plans for a new boat large enough to entice Evgenia to sail with him once more.

# Chapter Ten

# SECRET WATER

RANSOME REMAINED in the Norwich nursing home over Christmas and into the New Year, after which he was able to return home and make a start on the long-awaited pictures for *Swallows and Amazons*.

When Ransome visited Pin Mill to talk with Harry King who had been commissioned to build his new yacht, he was accosted by Mr Gee, the self-styled 'Mayor of Pin Mill', who demanded to know why Miss Powell had been put into *We Didn't Mean to Go to Sea* and not him. He was the local greengrocer who had his 'Mayor's Parlour' under the gable end of Alma Cottage. Had Ransome let out that he was one of that early list of minor characters?

The new boat was designed by a leading naval architect, Fred Shepherd, and Ransome took a keen interest during the months of its building in the shed where Harry King and his sons had established an enviable reputation for fine, honest workmanship. He haunted the boatyard and recorded every stage in the building in a draft for the book that would surely have appeared in due course to the delight of the yachting fraternity and his army of fans, but for World War Two that put an end to sailing for six years.

With his mind on the new boat, Ransome found

The cottage at Kirby Quay inhabited by the 'witch' in *Secret Water*.

Kirby (Witch's) Quay is a peaceful haven, seemingly miles from the outside world that is, in reality, only half a mile away.

it hard to concentrate on his next book. Once more he made up his mind that he had finished with the Swallows and Amazons — at least for the time being. He fancied the idea of 'another wild *Peter Duck* yarn', preferably on dry land! More tempting in its way, was a tale for which he had already sketched out 31 chapters — a Victorian tale 'about an old schoolmaster and a fisherman and a boy and a river' — but he did not feel the time was right, with everyone expecting another book for 'brats' quite apart from which, Evgenia was firmly against the idea.

As a devoted reader of Agatha Christie, Ransome was attracted by the idea of writing a detective story. He had fixed upon a villain, the detectives and the vague outline of a plot, but he

could not think of a crime. He appealed to Margaret Renold for ideas, and had she been able to suggest a suitable crime it is unlikely that *Secret Water* would have been written.

Meanwhile, he abandoned the *Swallows and Amazons* pictures for a time while he wrote 46 pages inspired by his recent fishing holiday on the Broads — 'a gorgeous episode with a pike, and a fisherman and an innkeeper and the Death and Glories' and 'Night Affair' about the Coot Club's visit to one of the few remaining old Broadsmen who kept body and soul together by catching eels.

He got no further with the Broads detective yarn and he went back to thinking about the beginnings of an idea that he had jotted down the previous August.

*Muddy creeks . . . tidal . . . an island . . . like Walton Backwaters . . .a hut . . . a house . . .*

*Town children come along . . . the Callums . . . Local children watch . . .*

*The visitors know they are being watched, but cannot see anybody . . .*

*The locals show themselves up when the visitors get into the Dickens of a mess, and are doing their best but failing to get out of it . . . In the end of course it is the locals who are in a mess and the visitors somehow help them through.*

This rough outline does not seem very much like *Secret Water*, but the next synopsis is called 'Marooned; or the Mastodon Boy'. While Commander Walker and his wife are busy moving into their new quarters in Shotley they maroon the rest of the family on an island where he had spent a weekend as a boy, given plenty of tinned food, a rope, an axe and a saw and left to fend for themselves.

Having settled in to their camp they explore the island and see huge mastodon footprints in the mud. Next morning, through the mist they see something moving on one of the other islands. They erect a flagstaff, and after the mist has cleared they see a small boy crossing the mud that has been left by the falling tide in order to reach the mainland. He is walking awkwardly with great duckboards attached to his feet to prevent him sinking deep into the mud. The boy leaves the duckboards at the water's edge and disappears inland.

Some time later that day when Roger is on watch, he spots the boy running 'like blazes' across some low ground on the mainland and then the boy vanishes. After a while they see what he is running away from when a boy and girl with a spaniel appear ('A blood hound', says Titty) but the chase ends when they come to the ditch where the boy disappeared. They watch the islanders for a bit and then go away. Presently they cross to the island in a duck punt, land and come ashore to the camp. They are very polite and seem friendly enough, but rather inquisitive looking into the Swallows tents. They say nothing about the boy that they were chasing and neither do the Swallows.

The others are hardly out of sight when the Mastodon appears and explains the reason for the chase. At this point Ransome admitted that this was more than he could! The Mastodon stays to supper and the next day at high water the Swallows swim across to his island. The Mastodon shows them his lair in the stern of a derelict barge, most of which is rotting away. He accepts their marooning and they accept his scheme (whatever it is) and they decide to join up to help one another.

The boy shows them how to lay out eel lines and after shooting is heard he brings a wild duck which has fallen on his island and Susan cooks it.

There is another chase in which Roger becomes a red herring playing the part of the mastodon boy and evades the pursuers by rolling in the ditch while they pass by.

There is some raft-building and the climax is reached when a high tide swamps their island. As the tide reaches the top of the sea wall they manage to take to the barely-completed raft and would have drifted out to sea had the mastodon boy not managed to throw them a rope. They are still on the raft when the Goblin arrives to take them off and finds the island swamped.

'All hopelessly vague,' wrote Ransome, 'but the business of the islands and the mastodon boy in his lair in the old barge does seem somehow promising.' Fragmentary notes show how the story began to take shape in Ransome's mind. There is a mention of a totem and the Mastodon looking hopefully at plump Bridget, whose eventual sacrifice is witnessed with horror by the 'enemies'. Sinbad makes peace with Sam the 'bloodhound', and the Mastodon brings Sinbad fresh milk instead of the Swallows' condensed.

Another page contains the suggestion that Nancy and Peggy arrive on the scene with a 'communication'.

Ransome summed up the plot simply, 'Not good enough. The enemies must get into difficulties and be saved by the mastodon boy ...witnessed by the Swallows. Then the Mastodon and the enemies must get into difficulties and be saved by the Swallows . . Some sort of dark climax of that kind is essential.

The enemies? Visitors with their own games to play trying to join up with the elusive Mastodon who, while avoiding them, accepts that the Swallows are genuinely marooned.'

It was still too vague and Ransome wisely left it there. Wren Howard was thinking of Christmas 1938 without a new Ransome book when he confided, 'It's a bit serious about the new book. Won't the Walton Creek idea work out at all? I liked the sound of the skeleton of it. In any case it ought to be possible, I think, to be more land than water this time, though a certain amount of water is always useful and exciting.'

Wren Howard was still fiercely chasing Ransome for the pictures, explaining that he was reprinting in small quantities in anticipation that they might yet turn up. At last, in November 1938 the 14th printing of *Swallows and Amazons* carried the author's illustrations, as had the eighth edition of *Swallowdale* the previous June. The *Swallows and Amazons* pictures were finished at the end of March in time for a holiday on the Broads, this time as Admiral to a fleet of five yachts crewed mostly by teenage friends who flew the skull and crossbones, enlivened their cruise with some mildly piratical activities, and amongst themselves referred to Ransome as 'Barnacle Bill'. Ransome noted that the smartest crew were the Coniston pirates, Taqui and Titty Altounyan.

There was plenty to occupy Ransome in the summer of 1938. He was free from financial worries and from the hateful (at times) business of doing his best work at the pace demanded by Jonathan Cape's annually rotating treadmill. At last he was able to indulge his love of boats, or simply being afloat and snuggled down in a peaceful anchorage.

He kept a detailed record of the building and launch of the new boat that they had decided to call *Selina King*. The *Nancy Blackett* was made ready for the summer as he confessed to feeling it would be unfair not to sail in the sturdy craft that he would not have thought of parting with, had Evgenia not demanded a 'yard-wide galley table', around which the new yacht would be designed! He arranged a second 'Whitsuntide' cruise to Burnham and Lowestoft with his staunch friend Philip Rouse. *Selina King* was not launched until the season was almost over and *Nancy Blackett* was not neglected after all. By the end of the summer, he had visited Kirby Creek five times, the River Deben twice and paid another visit to Burnham.

In an early weekend at Kirby Creek Philip Rouse and he took a dinghy and navigated the winding channel to Kirby Quay (Witch's Quay) — a piece of exploration that would eventually be used in the book — and the following day they searched for flints on the beach at Stone Point (Flint Island).

Real inspiration for 'Marooned' came at the beginning of September when Ransome had arranged to meet up with a 'fleet of pirates' in the Walton Backwaters in order to take some 'hollywoods'. These were the Busk family whom Ransome had met soon after arriving at Pin Mill. Their three youngsters enjoying themselves with splashing and laughter, having 'capsizing parties' had intrigued him. These were John (14) Gillian (13) and Michael (10). When he asked the boatmen what was going on, he was told to take no notice, it was only the Busks! Very soon they were all firm friends. Major Edmund Busk, M.C. was a rather reserved man who did not make friends easily — rather like Ransome, but their friendship endured until Ransome's death. The parents had their 30ft. gaff cutter *Lapwing* at anchor off Stone Point and the children were camping on Horsey (Swallow) Island. The family had arrived with a fairly blank map and were engaged in making a chart of the Backwaters. The parents and Michael, the youngest, sailed *Wizard* and they looked after the food, John and his cousin sailed *Zip* and Gillian and Major Busk's godson struggled with a dinghy that they had borrowed called *Jo*. After a morning of exploration they met at a pre-arranged spot and 'rafted-up' for lunch. There was more exploration in the afternoon before returning to base and comparing maps over the evening meal. After a day or two, the *Nancy Blackett* arrived with Ransome at the helm and George and Josephine hauling up the Jolly Roger. George and Josephine joined the camp ashore the following day and *Nancy Blackett* successfully circumnavigated Horsey Island, safely crossing The Wade at the top of the tide. Ransome took his 'hollywoods' and Gillian posed for the drawing of Peggy having her finger pricked.

The Busk youngsters were turned into Dum, Dee and Daisy, the Children of the Eel and savage blood brothers and sister of the Mastodon — although they in no way resembled them. Their yacht, *Lapwing*, appeared under its own name and when the book appeared it was dedicated to the Busk family.

Years later after the Second World War, Ransome was at Pin Mill with his yacht *Peter Duck*, and the object of attention by some young admirers. Seeing Gillian, who had taken a degree at Cambridge and was just out of uniform after service in the A.T.S., he told the children, 'There's Daisy. You go and ask her.' Gillian was not

The Wade in *Secret Water* at high tide appears to be an inland sea, but a few hours later the scene is very different.

Low water across the Wade. Lorries have successfully crossed but there is treacherous mud either side of the road.

*Nancy Blackett* is now owned by a charitable trust and makes regular appearances around the south and east coast harbours. Here her crew make all shipshape after returning to Levington Marina following a trip down the River Orwell.

impressed, never having felt in the least like Daisy and certainly not after six years of war. Evgenia had become adept at protecting Ransome from too much attention, but seems to have failed on this occasion.

The 'King of Horsey Island', David Haig-Thomas, an Olympic oarsman and Arctic explorer made a fleeting appearance in the book as the farmer who provided milk and conveyed messages for the explorers that had been marooned on his island.

That visit to Kirby Creek was the last time Ransome sailed *Nancy Blackett*, although it was not until well into November before he was able to

take *Selina King* to sea. He made short fishing trips until Christmas and on the day after Boxing Day he entered in the log, 'Come aboard 11.30. Lit fire. All dry and well. She is a grand ship.' It was almost as if Ransome could not keep away.

In December Ransome made a start on the book with the opening chapters, 'Farewell to Adventure', 'Into the Unknown' and 'Marooned'. After Christmas, he continued with the next couple of chapters, although he had no clear idea where the book was going, once Titty and Bridget have discovered mastodon prints in the mud.

The Oxford University Press asked Ransome to write 'A Book of Myths', but he turned it down. He had *Selina King* to prepare for the new season and the elusive plot of the new book to catch, and this left no time to think of myths even had he wanted to do so.

In the middle of January 1939 they decided to leave Broke Farm and move to the other side of the river in the hope of finding some peace and quiet. From the beginning of April they rented Harkstead Hall, a pleasant square brick farmhouse only a couple of miles from Pin Mill and close to the home of Major Busk with whom he enjoyed many a game of billiards.

At the beginning of March, Ransome went to Jonathan Cape's Bedford Square offices to discuss with Wren Howard what he had by way of a plot for 'Marooned'. He had decided that the Swallows should have a purpose rather than mere survival once they had been marooned. They would attempt to map the Walton Backwaters before they were 'rescued' and taken off. The girl, boy and their spaniel and referred to as 'the enemies', have been replaced more colourfully by 'The Children of the Eel'.

The Swallows would not be able to complete their map-making without a boat to explore the inland sea that would be as true to life as the Broads had been, rather than treated like the lake in the north.

Howard's reaction was to say, 'Go ahead.'

Ransome clarified the main motives in the story:

*Bridget — always on the look out for being done out of anything on account of her youth, this being her first time on an expedition with the others.*

*The Map — this is printed at intervals throughout the book, showing the gradual diminution of the unexplored areas.*

*Nancy — a bit jealous of the map for getting in the way of war and savagery.*

*The Mastodon — lovely at first waiting for the savages, then joyfully accepting the Ss and As, being carried off his feet by Nancy, and letting the lot of them into the secrets of the eel tribe. Then horrified by message from other savages warning him to have nothing to do with the strangers. Then finding that the other savages, on meeting the Ss and As behave exactly as he had done himself.*

The book progressed slowly throughout the spring, although it is not possible to follow its progress closely because Ransome's diary is full of *Selina King*. Once Howard had given him the go-ahead, he had written 54 pages by the end of the month. He managed only two pages in April, partly because he led the 'Northern River Pirates' on another Broads holiday afloat. He added 40 pages in May and a further 71 pages before the first draft was ready for a complete read-through on June 27th. Having done so, he was bothered by the ending. It was 'altogether weak'. The motives were 'cloudy' and much more background was needed. He needed to make more of the savages and the Mastodon.

The following day Ransome came up with a solution to the weak ending difficulty: Titty and Nancy, realising that they have in their different ways, prevented the map from being finished in time, decide separately to rise early and complete the exploration. When they wake in the morning, John, Susan and Bridget are alone in the camp and jump to the conclusion that the others have sloped off to have a final race..

A month later he had 432 pages of 'very rough copy' that was as 'flat as our drinking water'. Ransome went off to Paris for a couple of days while Evgenia read it through and while he was there he learnt of the secret service agent who was sent to prison in Finland in 1919 because the authorities thought that the poor man was Ransome. Evgenia was her usual damning self, but this time Ransome thought that he could put it right without too much difficulty.

On the day that war was declared, Ransome visited Pin Mill and found 'The Mayor' sitting at the top of the stairs in his gas mask during the practice air-raid warning. Almost at once he sought permission from the Royal Navy to sail *Selina King* to a place where she would be under cover, because Harry King's shed was too small to house the Pin Mill flotilla of little ships and might be required for war work.

A further period of extensive revision came to an end in mid-September when Wren Howard declared that he was 'very pleased' with the manuscript. He thought that by increasing the pace in the last few chapters Ransome had succeeded in keeping the interest alive to the end. He had found it a little difficult to follow without maps, but that would soon be remedied. Howard agreed with Ransome's forecast that the sale of children's books would not be affected by the outbreak of World War Two, although he thought that distribution might be more difficult. Cape had plenty of paper in hand, but there were fears that they might not be able to remain in the Bedford Square offices in central London and have to retire further out into the suburbs.

In his haste to complete the pictures Ransome drew the meal dial incorrectly and had to alter the position of the meal pegs for later editions.

At the end of September Ransome took *Selina King* for a final sail up the coast to Lowestoft, so that she could be laid up for the duration of the war under cover at Oulton Broad. It proved to be a hazardous voyage with a successful negotiation of the tricky Southwold entrance and the distressing sight of the masts of sunken ships showing above the waves.

*Secret Water* was published on November 28. As well as the 10,000 copies mentioned by Wren Howard, another three editions were published that month, amounting to a further 5,000 copies. The book was reviewed by an anonymous writer in *The Times Literary Supplement:*

*Once more the Swallows and Amazons have a magnificent exploring adventure, once more Mr. Arthur Ransome has kept a complete record of their experiences, terrors, triumphs and set it down with the cunning that casts a spell over new children and old each Christmas. In* Secret Water, *the intrepid band are marooned on an island by their father's orders aud instructed to stick it out for a week and not come ashore without making a complete map of the secret archipelago. Easier said than done because they are not alone on the island, hostile inhabitants threaten them, there is a mastodon's footprints in the mud and the Children of the Eel have to be placated. Bridget, the ship's baby is made prisoner, Titty is trapped by the tide,* but these resourceful and intelligent youngsters are by this time well able to apply their brains to any and every problem. Difficulties may discourage them for a time, but they are not to be daunted for long. Their tempers and training are tested severely, but, without being super children, they are quick-witted and trustworthy and they deserve the superb fun put their way by their Naval father and an accommodating mother, who has to swallow her qualms, when her seafaring brood grow restless.

*The child who longs to be an explorer and hasn't the luck of the Walkers will happily lose himself in this book and learn a lot of sense from it. Envy may set in later, when the last thrill has been tasted, but entertainment will prevail and a beautiful peace where this book is found.*

Unlike its predecessors, *Secret Water* was printed in Oxford at the Alden Press, a small family concern that had agreed to print only those books published by Cape. Together, Alden and Cape formed an excellent working relationship and this enabled Howard to leave much of the layout to the Alden typographers whom he knew he could trust. The Swallows and Amazons books had always been bound by A. W. Bain & Co, a company that had been bought by Cape in 1936 with proceeds from the hugely successful *Seven Pillars of Wisdom,* and for a time Cape probably produced the finest mass-produced books in the country. As with Alden, Cape's concern was with quality and speed of service. Most of the paper for Cape came from John Dickinson & Co with whom Cape had no financial interest, but by meeting Howard's specific requirements, Dickinson, Alden and Bain each played their part in giving Cape books their distinctive look and feel.

## Chapter Eleven

# THE BIG SIX

RANSOME CAME OUT of the Norwich nursing home in January 1938 with the outline of a detective story in his mind. He had, in George Owden, a ready-made villain with a grudge against the Coot Club. All the plot required was a crime that Owden could commit in order that all Horning would blame the Coots. Aided by Dorothea's imaginative mind and Dick's scientific

one, they would become the detectives. Port and Starboard who seem to have been invented for the purpose of hitching lifts in varied Broads craft in *Coot Club* have been packed off to Paris.

Ransome wanted to write a cold weather story because he had a 'gorgeous episode' with a pike, the Death and Glories, a fisherman and an innkeeper that was too good to waste. He thought it should take place in October or November, or even the week before Christmas. Cold weather would also give him the chance to have some fun with the old coal stove that the Death and Glories have fitted in the cabin of their old boat with its genuine earthenware chimney pot on the cabin roof. There would be a frightful episode when they attempt to smoke eels in their cabin and a good one when they have a Christmas pudding with mentholated spirit slopped over all to set it alight, and lots of sugar in an unsuccessful attempt to take the taste away.

**The attraction of the riverside village of Horning owes much to the 'bit of green grass' between the staithe and the shops.**

The unusual sight of three traditional yachts moored opposite Horning Staithe.

Another rare occasion – only two boats are moored by Horning Staithe.

Whatever the crime, it must be one that could be repeated, so that at the very end, after all their detective work, the detectives would catch George Owden in the act. With the thought of the *Margoletta* in *Coot Club* in mind, the villainy must not be anything to do with visitors' boats. Having explained this to Margaret and Charles Renold, Ransome concluded, 'Gosh, Margaret, if you can provide the right crime, I'll write you the loveliest detective story that ever was.'

Ransome did not begin his thriller until the middle of the 'phoney war'. He had come to the inevitable conclusion, that far from it being undesirable to have a crime in any way related to boats, in a place like Horning where a good proportion of the workforce were engaged in boatbuilding, it would be natural and cause any amount of bad feeling. If boats were cast off, the Coots would be blamed, as everybody in the village had heard the story of Tom and the *Margoletta*.

The new book had no name when he started work on chapter one on January 1st 1940. He wrote in the following order, dancing around forward and backwards in a way that shows that he had a very clear idea of the plot from the beginning. Many of the chapters have working titles, but it is possible to identify them as follows. — 'Quayside Scenes' 'Out of the Dentist's Window' (chapter 1), 'First Sign of Trouble' (2), 'Eel Sett at Night' (3), 'Misleading Appearances' (4), 'The First Clue' (14), 'What Happened to the Fish' (33), 'Blinding Flash' (28), 'Siege of the Death and Glory' (29), 'Darkening Clouds' (5), 'Money to Burn' (9), 'Breakfast at Dr Dudgeon's' (10), 'We Got to Emigrate' (11), 'Worse and Worse' (12), 'Two Ways of Looking at the Same Thing' (13), 'Rival Detectives' (14), 'A Scrap of Flannel' (18), 'Unwanted Gift' (19), 'A Kid for the Tiger' (26), 'Dunlop Tyres' (20), 'Morning Visitors' (21), 'Another Coat of Paint' (22), 'The Villain Leaves his Mark' (23), two chapters that Ransome called 'More Shades', and 'Bill?', 'Things look Black' (24), 'The Last Chance' (25), 'All the Evidence We Got' (30), 'Tow out of Trouble' (6), 'Spreading the Net' (16). These were followed by a revision of 'Eel Sett at Night', 'Misleading Appearances' and 'Smoked Eels'.

Missing from this list are: 'The World's Whopper' (7) and 'At the Roaring Donkey' (8) that had been written two years earlier, 'In the Dark Room' (31) and 'The Legal Mind' (32). The chapters 'Spreading the Net' (16) and 'News from the Outposts' (17) were added once the first draft was completed and they provide an interesting exercise in necessary but fruitless detective work.

Amazingly, Ransome had 401 pages of the first draft completed by April 27, compared with *Coot Club* on July 3rd, *Secret Water* on July 19th and *Winter Holiday* on August 9th.

The book progressed more rapidly than at any time since he had been composing episodes of *Peter Duck* to read to the Altounyans. There can be little doubt that the enthusiasm that shone from his letter to Margaret Renold two years earlier was sweeping him along. 42 pages had been written in 1938, a further 80 were added in January, 107 in February, 101 in March and 71 in April.

A couple of pages of his unrevised 1938 chapters have survived. The story of Joe waking the President of the Coot Club so that they can go to the eelman's together is written from the point of view of Tom. After he has been sleeping for three hours he has a dream.

*His father and another doctor were arguing about his foot.*

*'Not worth keeping,' said his father.*

*'They never are when they turn into cactuses,' said the other doctor. 'You hold it steady while I saw. He won't feel it sleeping like that.'*

*'Ow. Won't I?' said Tom.*

*Something sharp was cutting into his ankle. Tom pulled his foot away and made the pain worse. Then, awake, he struggled down under the bedclothes to get hold of the string.*

When Tom gives the password, 'Coots for ever,' Joe responds with the amusing countersign 'Baldheaded'.

The episodes that had been written in advance of a plot were ingeniously slotted into the story so that they provide a change of pace and at the same time move the plot forward. Ransome seems to have been quite content to allow the reader to guess the identity of the villain from the beginning, for the book tells the story of the Coots' efforts to clear their name. The suspense builds until it seems that nothing can prevent the 'wrongful arrest' of the Death and Glories. It takes the detectives some days before the intuitive Dorothea realises that crimes were only the means by which George Owden planned to see that the river would

The Wilderness above Horning Ferry in the 1930s with the new bungalows and the wind pump mentioned in *The Big Six*.

The road beside the Wilderness where George Owden left his bicycle tracks. More and more building and dyke-cutting has transformed the place and only the strip beside the road remains undeveloped.

Some neat bungalows have been built along the bank of the River Thurne not far from the scene of the capture of the World's Whopper.

The view up Horning Town Reach towards the staithe and the Swan Inn has changed little in the last seventy years. The boatshed where Joe thought he saw the flash of the villain's torch in *The Big Six* is on the extreme right.

The River Bure looking downstream on a misty morning, photographed from close to the place where Dr. Dudgeon's home would have been.

be free of bird protectors the following nesting season.

When the Death and Glories are seeking a suitable sanctuary somewhere near the village of Horning yet off the main river, there is an interesting reference to the fact that *The Big Six* took place in September 1933, when Ransome explains that some building has recently taken place on what was the Wilderness — as indeed it had! Similarly, the drainage ditch over which Bill moves the plank had been widened by 1938, probably to allow access to the newly-built Ferry

Boatyard. Already the stories of the Swallows and Amazons and their friends were becoming period pieces.

After a break of a fortnight Ransome began the second typescript, encouraged by Evgenia's unusually favourable verdict that the framework was even better than *We Didn't Mean to Go to Sea*. She had found two good chapters and the book had made her laugh several times. He told Wren Howard that he had started on the revision of 'Hot Water', 'Not Us', 'Coots in Trouble' 'Who the Michief?' — or 'God knows what', although he was not satisfied with any of these titles. Unless 'Hitler, that illiterate bloke' should 'butt in' with an invasion before the revision was complete, he thought that he could have it ready for the end of June!

Ransome gave the Death and Glories the same diet of bread, cheese and apples on which he had existed when he was a struggling writer. There can be no doubt that he was enjoying the writing, for the word 'fun' occurs in several letters about his work, rather than the 'bilge' which had cropped up from time to time in the past.

Among the fan letters at that time came one from a young American, enquiring if the Swallows and Amazons were being evacuated to America and hoping that they would be allowed to stay together.

Ransome had been rather too optimistic about the completion date, for he was only half-way through the revision by the end of June. For this delay the developing war in the air was largely responsible, as the Battle of Britain was about to start. Daily sirens, 'baying like wolves with stomach aches' unsettled Ransome who was becoming hypersensitive to unwelcome noise. During his short stay at Harkstead Hall he complained to the village school nearby about the noise the children made during playtime. Eventually, in old age, he would be remembered by a river-keeper as 'a grumbly old bugger'.

For a time they thought of moving to London, and they would have done so if his mother could have found them a small house in a really quiet neighbourhood. Shortly afterwards his mother left her house in Kew and moved in with her sister at Seend in Wiltshire, and they thought very seriously of taking it over. It was just as well that they did not do so, for they would have found the blitz intolerable. Meanwhile there was a serious doubt about their continued tenure of Harkstead Hall, as the house was liable to be commandeered for the military at any time. This uncertainty, and the misery of nights disturbed by sirens and gunfire was enough to make Evgenia finally agree to a move back to the Lake District, under certain conditions — indoor sanitation, water supply, electricity etc. By the time they came to leave Harkstead she had only managed four nights of unbroken sleep in as many months. Ransome was always able to take pleasure in little things — he carefully drew some unusual caterpillars that he found in the garden and watched over a pair of wagtails nesting in the creeper outside his window — but being unable to sail or use the car, and with his young friends in uniform, there was little to keep him in Suffolk. Colonel Busk had been recalled to the War Office and his elder son John had lost his life when serving aboard *HMS Norfolk*.

Meanwhile Ransome was having a tussle with Howard over the title. Cape wanted 'The Death and Glories' which Ransome thought had warlike connotations and he much preferred the rather obscure title 'The Big Six'. In the end he had his way, although it was necessary to put an explanation on the title page. In reality, 'The Big Five' were the Chief Inspectors who were well known as the senior detectives at New Scotland Yard who were called in to help with complicated murder cases in other parts of the country and abroad.

Ransome responded to the Broadland rivers almost as strongly as he did the lake country, and among the charms of *The Big Six* are striking evocations of time and place.

*Bill moved to that brighter window and looked out. There was a glow in the eastern sky. Down river the water shone silver with splashes of green. The dawn was climbing, putting out the stars.*

*The morning mist was heavy on the river and on the sodden fields that lay on either side of it. The fields were below the level of the river and the Death and Glories, marching along the rond that kept the river from overflowing, looked down on feeding cattle and horses whose coats were pale with moisture.*

*An old bream turned with a quiet splash somewhere out on the river and Pete listened for it to splash again. He heard a rabbit stamping the ground and all but pressed the button, but guessed what it was in time. He heard, far away in the meadows below the level of the river, the lumbering tread of the old horse. He heard a car on the road Ludham way. That light in the sky must be over Yarmouth. Something small ran close by him. One of them old rats.*

On July 23rd the second draft was posted to

Howard, and Ransome turned his attention to the drawings and covered 40 pages of his sketchbook with preliminary sketches. He told his mother that he had found that drawing concentrated his mind and that it was a good way of dealing with the worsening wartime situation. Two of the most interesting show cross-sections of the *Death and Glory* showing the three small boys on board. Ransome had measured and drawn an old ship's lifeboat in his pocket book at some time, and he used these measurements to show the *Death and Glory* as a cabin boat. The finished pictures contain some of his best work, and the study of the pike deep in the river drew warm praise from his mother. It is interesting to see the way that Ransome's drawing had matured, by comparing the frontispiece 'At the Staithe' with a similar picture 'On Horning Staithe' in *Coot Club*.

It is probable that Ransome never got around to drawing maps for *The Big Six*, as the endpaper maps are identical to *Coot Club's* front endpaper of the Northern Rivers, and the excellent map of the River Bure near Horning is a revised and enlarged version of the one in the earlier book.

As The Battle of Britain reached its climax in September came the news that the blocks for the illustrations had been lost when the works received a direct hit, the day after the blockmaker had finished them. Fortunately the original drawings had been in the post on their way back to Cape, and Howard was still optimistic that *The Big Six* would be out by Christmas. Unfortunately when they started to make the replacement blocks they found that some drawings had been lost after all. Bombs had dropped close to Bedford Square and the publishers had lost some of their windows. The staff at Jonathan Cape had retired to the basement but they were determined to keep going, even though they were going to have to restrict their list to 'safe' books — including the Swallows series.

At the end of September they heard of a possible house at Coniston that they both knew and liked, and before the family could advise against a return to the Lake District, Ransome had travelled by train to the north and all had been arranged. As his mother wryly pointed out, her son had something to thank Hitler for at last!

By the beginning of October the Ransomes were installed in their new home. The Heald is a bungalow close to the road running along the eastern side of Coniston Water that was about 20 years old at that time. Having bought it, Ransome became a minor landowner with half a mile of lake frontage and 17 acres of woodland. They had two sitting rooms, a kitchen, a modern bathroom and three small bedrooms, generated electricity and central heating.

Ten days later the Ransomes drove up to the Lake District where they were welcomed at High Hollin Bank by Barbara, Oscar and Janet Gnosspelius, and Ursula Collingwood with her husband and the Kelsalls who had all come across from Troutbeck. That night they slept in the great barn at High Hollin Bank, only a mile or two from The Heald, and the following day with the help of Barbara and Janet they moved in.

Ransome was delighted to be back beside the lake that he loved, and for a while was in seventh heaven. The replacement drawings were quickly attended to, and somehow Cape managed to have the picture proofs ready for October 21st. In spite of everything, Wren Howard was still determined that come what may, the blitz over London was not going to stop *The Big Six* from being in the shops in time for Christmas. His tenacity and the efforts of Cape's printers, binders and distributers were rewarded. *The Big Six* was published at the end of November and in three weeks had sold a rewarding 9 400 copies of the 12 000 that had been printed.

By this time, Ransome's royalties had increased from 10% to 20% as a mark of the success of the Swallows and Amazons books. In return, Ransome contemplated leaving any royalties that would fall due after their deaths, to the publishers. Tabitha would not receive a penny, after she continued to withhold his library following the death of Ivy earlier that year, although she did offer to sell it to him. When Ransome ignored the letter, she disposed of the books for a pittance and he bought back from the purchaser some of his early notebooks that she had no right to sell. It was clearly an illogical matter of principle, since he had long ago ceased to need his library in order to write, and had become, as Evgenia put it, someone who 'made books out of their head'. Cape increased the price from 7/6 to 8/6 and later 9/-, but continued to base his royalties on the pre-war price as a wartime measure. This arrangement continued well into the nineteen fifties, by which time Ransome calculated that he had lost some £10,000 — and that was the end of the suggestion of a bequest to Cape.

Looking upstream a few seconds
before the photograph on page 125.

This converted ship's boat could be seen along the
river near Horning until a few years ago. The
resemblance to the *Death and Glory* is remarkable.

Arthur Ransome: Master Storyteller

The notice board beside Horning Staithe where Rodleys 'papered' Tom Dudgeon, and Farland, Farland and Farland 'papered' the Death and Glories offering a reward for conviction.

Ransome's mother received one of the earliest copies without the familiar montage dust jacket, but it seems that the problem with the drawings was resolved before the main first edition printing that was clothed in a colourful crimson and white cover.

Reviewing the book for *The New York Times*, Mary Eaton wrote:

*Out of war-torn England (the author's drawings were destroyed by one bomb, the publisher's plates removed by another and the proofs lost at sea) comes a new Arthur Ransome story, as fresh in interest, as perceptive and true in values as all the others.*

After outlining the plot Mary Eaton concludes:

*These are real children drawn by one who has watched boys and girls with wisdom, sympathy and humour, one who enjoys and understands them. The schemes of the Big Six for catching the wrongdoers have the same mixture of practical good sense and make-believe that is found in the doings of children in real life.*

After the gritty realism of The Big Six it was almost inevitable that Ransome should turn to romantic adventure, but it is unlikely that anybody would have predicted that the Swallows and Amazons would end up as the prisoners of a Latin-spouting female Chinese pirate!

# Chapter Twelve

# MISSEE LEE

WHEN RANSOME WROTE JOYFULLY to tell Wren Howard that he was once more a Lake District landowner, he added confidently that it would mean a fresh lot of lake country Swallows and Amazons. However, both Cape and his American publisher, Macmillan, urged him to write another *Peter Duck* style romance that would make a change from the realism of his other stories. Ransome himself had been hankering after such a tale ever since *We Didn't Mean to Go to Sea*.

Furthermore, Howard appealed to Ransome to avoid the war at all costs. It was not that Cape was against war stories as such — Mary Treadgold's story of escape from the Nazi occupied Channel Isles, *We Couldn't Leave Dinah* was published alongside *Missee Lee*. Very likely the astute Howard recognised that the Swallows and Amazons were too firmly rooted in the innocent days of the early nineteen-thirties to be transplanted into wartime.

The result was a much more original and distinguished successor to *Peter Duck*. It was a true successor, in that the Swallows are the same as they were in *Peter Duck*, and not the Swallows of post-*We Didn't Mean to Go to Sea*. Bridget had served her purpose in bringing a younger perspective and light relief into *Secret Water* and was not needed — more is the pity!

On their voyage around the world the *Wild Cat* catches fire off the coast of China. Captain Flint and the Swallows and Amazons are swept ashore in their boats, only to be captured by pirates who inhabit three islands somewhere on the coast of China. Their chief turns out to be Taicoon Missee Lee, a young Cambridge-educated she-pirate who yearns to return to her studies. Miss Lee seizes the opportunity to have her own class of students learning Latin under her tutelage. Captain Flint complicates matters by saying that he is the Lord Mayor of San Francisco, but eventually all are together again, and somewhat unwillingly learning Latin. Just as the other taicoons are about to do away with the prisoners, Miss Lee arranges their escape aboard her private junk during the Dragon Festival. Miss Lee herself stows away aboard her own vessel and only emerges from hiding in order to save the *Shining Moon* from being wrecked and her crew drowned. She finally realises that she cannot carry out her plan of returning with them to Cambridge because her strong sense of duty to her father tells her that her proper place is the Three Islands.

Ransome's first thought was to begin his yarn after the *Wild Cat* has been wrecked and the crew have taken to a mixture of rafts and barrels. They allow Polly to fly off, and when she does not return Roger says that it means that they must be near land... It was Evgenia who suggested a Chinese background with Roger getting into trouble for interfering with a Chinese prayer-wheel. This became the episode when Roger adds an amusing end to a Latin rhyming warning in Miss Lee's dictionary lifted from Herbert Hanson's *Cruising Association Handbook*:

> 'Hic liber est meus
> Testis est dues
> Si quis furetur
> Per collum pendator
> Like this pore cretur'

was followed by an amusing drawing of the 'pore cretur' hanging from a gibbet.

'Herbert J. Hanson, O.B.E., scholar and seaman' was an old friend and he became *Missee Lee's* dedicatee.

The most important creation was the young woman that Ransome called 'a tough but a darling': a 'Chinese she pirate ... good English ... missionary educated ... and graduated from an American university.'

When Ransome went to China in 1927 — a visit that he did not particularly enjoy — he can have had no idea of the use to which he would put his time there. Out of his first-hand experiences came the part-inspiration for Miss Lee herself, the pirate chiefs, the Dragon Feast and lots of background detail. Miss Lee had several real-life female pirate forerunners. Her kidnapping exploits, ransom demands and protection racket are remarkably like those of the diminutive Lai Choi San, with her ever-present amahs (servants), black trousers and cartridge belt. At the time of Ransome's visit, she was known as 'The Queen of the Macao Pirates' and she continued her piratical misdeeds up to the Second World War. Lai Choi San had inherited a fleet of seven armed junks on the death of her father in 1922 and 'acquired' a further five. Her crews were powerful bare-chested giants with wide-brimmed hats. She was immortalised in the book by an American journalist, Aleko Lilius, *I sailed with Chinese Pirates*.

Missee Lee, the tiny unquestioned leader of her band of piratical Chinese and torn between

**Rosamond Soong Ching-ling**

**Sketch for 'The Little Dragon leaves the Yemen'**

Jan. 1. 1944

her longing for a career of scholarship in Cambridge and her duty to her father, was a much more complex character than Lai Choi San. The other source of inspiration was Soong Ching-ling whom he met in 1927, the daughter of a missionary and the widow of Sun Yat-sen, one of the leaders of the Chinese revolution. She was described by Ransome as 'a very charming young woman, an enthusiast'. Soong Ching-ling was educated in Shanghai and at university in America. She eventually became the first woman Chairman and later President of the People's Republic of China.

In the story, the Swallows, Amazons and Captain Flint are having a high old time sailing the *Wild Cat* on a round-the-world cruise. Reaching their hundredth port on an unidentified island off the coast of China (Ransome had an idea that it

Arthur Ransome's wartime retreat at The Heald with its 17 acres of woodland and half a mile of Coniston Water shore. Unfortunately it was not large enough for their needs and was sold as soon as the end of the war was in sight.

might be from Singapore or Hainan. Later he changed it to somewhere in the Dutch East Indies) they are jokingly warned to steer clear of Missee Lee. They are becalmed a couple of days later and while they are transferring petrol to the working tank, Gibber manages to set the schooner on fire. They take to the boats as the *Wild Cat* begins to burn. *Swallow* and *Amazon* become separated in the dark and have different adventures before they all end up on the coast of China as prisoners.

*Missee Lee* was started on New Year's Day 1941 with an amusing sketch of the great head of a carnival dragon with a pair of marching legs showing beneath. After a fortnight, Ransome continued in fits and starts until the middle of February. The plot would not come together for him and his jotted notes suggest some of the possible developments that were later discarded ... Miss Lee and the children smuggle themselves out of the Canton River and could arrive at Hong Kong in the dark, or work their way out to sea and be picked up by a passing steamship . . . Miss Lee having decided that Captain Flint was a very uncultured man and therefore of no interest to her, passes him over to one of her chieftains. Captain Flint then escapes and heads back to her stronghold where the Amazons were being held captive. But there was a problem about this. How would the imprisoned Captain Flint know where the Amazons were being held? . . . The Swallows could draw attention to themselves by singing 'Spanish Ladies'. . . Should the Dragon Procession provide a means of escape? Could Captain Flint and the children go wandering into the woods and seize Miss Lee's little junk? They would cast off and drift down the river towards the dangerous rapids. Miss Lee has been reading Horace on board and she makes her presence known as they reach the rapids, takes the tiller and steers them out to sea. . . Perhaps the Shining Moon could link up with Captain Walker in Malta?

To make the whole thing work, he decided he had to make the other pirate chieftains 'genuine villains'. By the end of February Ransome had reached 87 pages — half as many as *The Big Six* had reached by the same time. Instead of pressing on, Ransome wrote to Margaret and Charles Renold pleading for suggestions for another Lake District Swallows and Amazons, because Miss Lee was 'in extremis'. 'She is too fantastic to be done before she has properly rooted herself in reality,' he complained, even after he had 'wasted' six weeks on her, but perhaps he could still be in time for Christmas if another story was started without delay. 'My old brain is truly bust and wore out . . . it can run to headaches but not yarns.' Charles Renold responded with the suggestion of a story about evacuees, but Ransome, mindful of the directions of Cape, decided that he really had no alternative but to continue with 'Poor Miss Lee'.

Ransome was, of course, quite wrong. *Missee Lee* is the most original of the entire series. Victor Watson, who has made a study of children's literature, has gone so far as to call the book 'one of the greatest children's books of the century — a thriller-romance set in a distant, exotic place, vividly and economically described, among strange and ferocious people'.

Life at The Heald during the winter of 1941 was not the idyll that Ransome had naively anticipated. They both went down with influenza, there was a period when snow had blocked the road so that they were unable to use the car, and they discovered that the generator that provided their electricity supply was unreliable. The 'Gnossies' at High Hollin Bank were close by, but they could not be reached by signalling in the way that they had kept in contact with the Kelsalls at Low Ludderburn. In practice, it was discovered that The Heald was actually more isolated than Low Ludderburn. Petrol was strictly rationed and shopping and lunch at Ulverston every Tuesday involved a drive of almost thirty miles, while the village of Coniston was five miles away round the head of the lake, and at home any plans that Evgenia might have had to improve the garden seemed doomed to fail because of the regular visits of marauding sheep. Shopping for other essentials became a problem, and Ransome could not find the new pair of breeches that he badly needed.

In spite of these difficulties 'Poor Miss Lee' was progressing. At the centre of the book is the character of Miss Lee herself and her 'Cambridge' study in the heart of her stronghold where she presides over the daily Latin lessons. Ransome appealed to Margaret Renold for information about a girl student's first term at Cambridge. His letter shows that he had formed a very clear picture of the character of Miss Lee whom he thought would have been at Girton College. The story had a 'Lovely head . . . elegant tail . . .but suet pudding in the middle'. 'Quick QUICK . . .QUICK . . . QUICK!!' he urged.

Miss Lee's Robin Hood principle of only taking rich prisoners is not shared by her second in command and greatest rival, Taicoon Chang who was based on the formidable Chang Tsung-chang 'several inches over six feet high, a giant among the Chinese'. Taicoon Chang says 'rob the poor. More of them. Small profits and quick returns.' Another important Chinese was Miss Lee's old Counsellor who had served her father before her and who quotes Confucius at her. He seems to have been based on General Wu Pie-fu, 'an ancient-minded man', a poet and Confucian scholar who was a major war-lord.

Margaret Renold responded gamely to the many and various queries that Ransome hurled at her about Latin grammar and in order that Miss Lee's Newnham College background would be completely accurate. Miss Lee's Cambridge college became Newnham when he discovered that Margaret's friend Lady Barlow had been a student there. He would have liked to have Miss Lee bring her rudder to China to hang on her wall (she had coxed Newnham's second boat) but was told that the boat club was too hard up at the time that Miss Lee would have been a student to allow that sort of thing. Nevertheless she was able to have china ornaments, matchstands and vases with the

Newnham crest in her English sitting room.

Margaret was asked to help by providing samples of educated female handwriting for Miss Lee to anticipate her future academic career on the flyleaf of her Latin grammar. Did he really need them or was he involving his friends for fun? Apparently none of the samples were satisfactory and according to her daughter Janet, it was Barbara Gnosspelius who produced the desired signatures. Although some charming and accomplished drawings appear from time to time in Ransome's sketchbooks, illustrating poses or simply showing a variety of hats or feet, and there are various records of Ransome requesting help with this or that, it is very unlikely that any of the inked drawings included any of her work.

On his visit to China in 1927 it is very doubtful if Ransome took his camera, for he started to bombard his friends with requests for pictures of the Chinese riding donkeys showing their unusual saddles, pictures of chopsticks, pictures showing Chinese natural history, of mangoes, bamboos, Chinese clothing — even houses.

By the middle of May the draft was ready for Evgenia. Her verdict was welcomed by Wren Howard. 'I am far from depressed by the Verdict on the first draft of 'Miss Lee'. For it to be admitted that the actual skeleton of the book is much better than most of the others, and it contains two good chapters strikes me as being a tremendous advance on some of the things I have heard in past years!'

Ransome's optimistic claim that it would be impossible for Evgenia to overwork herself at The Heald proved to be way off the mark. In the summer they considered taking a holiday on a farm at Blawith near the foot of Coniston Water but in the end they stayed at home, much to the dismay of Ransome's mother who thought that they both badly needed a good rest.

The hard work on the revision was over by the end of July when the final draft was sent to Howard, and work began on the pictures. 'I cannot draw', he groaned to Margaret Renold as he worked on the 73 pages of preliminary sketches, repeating his request for 'trees and Chinks and donkeys, water kongs, costumes and what not'. Ransome had won the struggle for the title of *The Big Six*, but this time Cape prevailed, and 'Poor Miss Lee' became 'Missee Lee' — much to Ransome's disgust.

For some years only the combination of plenty of milk, a supply of which was always carried with him together with some biscuits, and the avoidance of aluminium cooking pots had been keeping Ransome going, and when there was a scare that milk would be rationed one winter there were real fears for his health. Fortunately it proved to be a false alarm.

Wren Howard sent a congratulatory telegram when he received the proofs: FINISHED PROOFS MIDNIGHT stop CONGRATULATIONS TWENTY-TWO GONG STORY stop MUCH PREFER ORIGINAL ENDING AND PROPOSE TO SEND MANUSCRIPT TO PRINTER. Howard thought that CONGRATULATIONS NUMPA ONE FIRST CHOP STORY would be too confusing for the G.P.O.! What remains unclear is whether the printed version is the 'original'. Perhaps Ransome sent two versions of the ending. The tone of a later letter from Howard suggests that it is: 'I have honestly enjoyed reading every word of the book and finding such a crop of Ransome subtleties. The other thing that struck me was that the illustrations are particularly in tune with the text and really illustrate it'.

Not everything illustrated the text, for some eagle-eyed Brownie patrol found no fewer than eight errors in Captain Flint's semaphore S.O.S. 'Curse and confound Captain Flint. It isn't the first time that fellow's carelessness has got me into trouble. . .What's the good of my taking trouble, when he goes and lets me down like this?'

Jonathan Cape put in an accompanying note with Ransome's royalty statement that October to comment on the general uniformity of the sales. *The Big Six*, being the latest and *Swallows and Amazons* as the first, naturally had the biggest sales, but he could not understand the difference in sales between *Winter Holiday* and *Pigeon Post*.

An astonishing 20 500 copies were printed in time for publication on December 5th. The paper in the first edition is thinner and the cover is of a different, slightly shiny cloth of a similar green colour. The combination of Dickenson's paper, printing by the Alden Press and binding by Bain and Co had been replaced by 'Printed in Great Britain by Butler and Tanner, Frome and London'.

As 1941 drew to an end, Ransome was considering buying a light motorcycle, although the local garage told him that he would have to wait until the following March.

# Chapter Thirteen

# THE PICTS AND THE MARTYRS

## or

## Not Welcome at All

IN AUGUST 1941, even before *Missee Lee* was at the printers, Wren Howard and Macmillan had begun to press for another, just as soon as Ransome could produce it. All that Ransome had in mind at that time was a vague idea of bringing back the Great Aunt from *Swallowdale*: Captain Flint takes his sister off on holiday leaving Nancy and Peggy in charge of Beckfoot. The Great Aunt comes to hear of this and with obvious displeasure announces that she will come to Beckfoot to take charge.

It was a sound notion. A return to the north country would re-energise the series after the exotic and retrospective *Missee Lee* and six years away from the magical lake. Readers could be relied upon to give the book a warm welcome for that reason alone, and the book's domestic simplicity and innocence, coming in the middle of the Second World War, was a reminder of more simple and happier days. Swallows' enthusiasts might regret their absence, but Ransome knew exactly what he was doing.

Three months later he had developed the idea a little further. Beginning on New Year's Day, Ransome really applied himself to the first draft, averaging five pages a day and had reached 121 pages by the end of the month. He was bothered about starting without establishing the details of the story and felt it would probably lead to an awful mess. February was an equally productive month and on one memorable day Ransome completed 10 pages! Then on March 5th he became firmly stuck, having reached page 259 of 'rough squish'. On March 23rd he complained to Charles Renold, 'I wish I had another wild *Peter Duck* or *Missee Lee* plot. The new book with strictly domestic interest is damnable. I hate it and so will everyone else.'

In a rough draft Ransome sketched out some ideas: Captain Flint has taken Mrs Blackett off on a jaunt to Madeira leaving Nancy Peggy and old Cook at Beckfoot preparing for Dick and Dorothea who are to stay at Beckfoot. The GA writes to say that she is sure that their mother would have asked her to stay if she had not thought it was imposing too much, and she felt it her duty to come to Beckfoot at once. Beckfoot is thrown into turmoil. Nancy decides that the GA must not be allowed to spoil the D's holiday and that they must come just the same and keep out of the way of the GA. The arrival of the D's is followed by their new boat that has come by rail. The D's camp in the wood (coppice?) by Beckfoot and a secret harbour is cut in the reeds in the Octopus Lagoon.

Life at Beckfoot becomes complicated. The GA asks for an apple tart that has been passed on to the D's, she complains that Cook is using too much milk and wasting meat. Old cook is about to explode. The whole countryside becomes involved in keeping the D's presence secret— the postman, milk boy, rector etc... because they all realise that the GA is already angry with Mrs Blackett for allowing Nancy and Peggy to remain at Beckfoot alone, and she would have more to complain about if she were to find out about the visitors.

Eventually the GA becomes suspicious and tries to catch Nancy and Peggy out when she thinks that they have gone somewhere that she has forbidden. Remembering what had happened two summers earlier, she goes to Swainsons Farm, but her nieces are not there. She is rowed across to Wild Cat Island by Mary Swainson, but they are not there either, and finally on to the houseboat that has been lent to Timothy in Captain Flint's absence. Seeing a note left for him, she assumes that it is for Nancy and Peggy and she decides to wait aboard, and of course becomes marooned there when Mary Swainson rows away.

Meanwhile, Timothy and the others have met

Brown Howe, one of several possible Beckfoots to be found around the shores of Coniston Water, appeared in the 1974 film of *Swallows and Amazons*.

Townhead near the foot of Windermere, has the look of Beckfoot as well as the possibility of suggesting a name chosen for its play with words.

Many years ago, Evgenia told me that the best way to find Darien, the Beckfoot Promontory and Horseshoe Cove was to drift around Windermere in a boat. She was right, as it is very easy to miss this Beckfoot Promontory on the western shore unless you keep close in.

The Dogs' Home (left) deep in the woods to the east of Coniston Water is another place of pilgrimage for Ransome enthusiasts.

The Dogs' Home interior (above) looks as if it has been whitewashed at some time. Above the door are the remains of some mysterious beams. Did the little place have some sort of loft at one time?

up ashore and he never goes back to the houseboat. When the Great Aunt does not return to Beckfoot there is a general hunt. Eventually, Dick and Dorothea are the ones that find and rescue her.

So far so good, but the climax had to make it seem credible that the GA would leave a note making it clear that it had been all right to leave Nancy and Peggy alone at Beckfoot. At the same time something must occur to the GA that produces 'a touch of pity for her in the hearts of the young savages'.

On another page entitled 'Aunt Helen's Suggestion' there is another attempt. In spite of good intentions the Amazons are late home one day and the GA, remembering what happened two years previously, thinks that they must be at Swainson's Farm. After sending for a driver, she gives chase in rattletrap, but the car runs out of petrol after a mile or so and while the man returns on foot to fetch a can, the GA impatiently sets out on foot, taking what she believes is a short cut through the woods and she becomes lost. The GA is discovered by a charcoal burner (or labourer or his wife) and taken to their nearby cottage. She orders someone to go and fetch the car, but they refuse, as nobody can leave the cottage for long because someone or other is ill. When the book was finally published it was dedicated to 'Aunt Helen' — a 'Certificated Fist Class Aunt'!

Among the treasures in the Abbot Hall Museum archive in Kendal is a complete synopsis for *The Picts and The Martyrs* entitled 'Great Aunt'. Sadly it is undated, so that it is not possible to trace the development of the plot with any accuracy. In the synopsis the boat has acquired a name, *Scarab*, but there is no mention of 'picts' or 'martyrs'. The short chapter 'Pigeons for Timothy' and the delightful 'Tickling Trout' are later additions, together with the two pages devoted to Nancy's return to Beckfoot in the thunderstorm.

Otherwise, there are only minor differences from the final version.

In chapter two 'The Visitors Arrive', they all walk down from the station to the boatbuilders in Rio Bay rather than catching the bus. In chapter six 'She's Here!' the D's walk down to the lake shore thinking of their new boat. On the way back they hear a low whistle and Nancy, who has slipped out in the dusk, tells them about the lookout spot from the top of the Beckfoot promontory. The following chapter about life at Beckfoot on the first morning of the GA's visit was cut when Ransome decided to make the viewpoint of the D's the main focus, so that life at Beckfoot was (with one exception) presented at secondhand through reports from Nancy, Peggy and Cook. The Amazons put up posts to act as leading marks so the D's can find the cut channel leading to the harbour in the lagoon. For a time Ransome toyed with the idea of a Lake District rainy day washing out the D's camp in the woods, and forcing them into the room with the bench and vice beneath the pigeon loft in the Beckfoot yard.

When he picked up the tale once more he added another 26 pages by the end of March. By the beginning of May he had more or less finished the first draft when he left for London to see a specialist about his hernia.

Already life at The Heald had lost almost all its appeal. His infirmity and a shortage of petrol had made him practically housebound in a bungalow that they found a terrible squash after Harkstead Hall, and true to form, Evgenia managed to overwork. Eventually Ransome managed to get hold of a motor-bike that he called 'The Monster' and was able to travel a little further afield. Did Evgenia ever ride pillion? We shall never know.

On one memorable occasion Ransome shot a deer in his wood. After careful stalking, he managed to despatch it cleanly, and immediately wished he had not fired. It was a little roe deer, but even so Ransome had great difficulty getting the carcass down to the road, and perhaps it was this struggle that precipitated his hernia. They ate the kidneys the same night and the liver the following day. 'Braithwaite' skinned it and cut it up and on Sunday, the Ransomes, the 'Gnossies', the Braithwaites and the farmer who sent their milk, all dined off venison.

His doctor forbad fell-walking and rowing and insisted that he should fish quietly from the bank in future. For a while Ransome did as he was told, but years later, at the age of 72, he was still wading chest-high in the River Leven whilst fishing for salmon.

Towards the end of June Ransome explained to Wren Howard that he was being held together with 'artificial pads and props' that prevented him from doing most of the things that he enjoyed. By now the working title 'Great Aunt' had become 'Picts and Martyrs'. The first draft had been 'ghastly' but the first 100 pages of the second were a little better. He anticipated that the total length of 350 pages would make a book a little shorter than *Missee Lee*, and he feared that he would still have to produce the usual 20 pictures. It was the sort of thing that could not be rushed, but he was dutifully plodding along. He claimed all along that he was persevering because the American edition would earn dollars and so contribute to the war effort.

The setting of *The Picts and The Martyrs* is the same enchanted land that had become familiar to readers of the four earlier books — The lake, Rio, Beckfoot and the Amazon River, Octopus Lagoon, High Topps, Tyson's Farm, Swainsons and the Houseboat. The boundary was pushed a little further north with the addition of the river at the head of the lake and the village beyond. In the woods not far from The Heald is an old stone hut with no glass in its window. This is one lakes' location about which there can be no debate, for it is exactly like The Dogs' Home that for ten days becomes the D's refuge at the centre of the story.

The second draft was completed at the end of July and one copy was sent to Wren Howard while the other was left for Evgenia to read while Ransome went south to Droxford in Hampshire for a couple of days fishing with a friend. Howard read his copy, liked it, and went off on holiday secure in the knowledge that he would not be spending August trying to prise the manuscript from his perfectionist author.

Ransome returned to London to find a letter from Evgenia waiting for him in Cape's office. It was a long letter in which Evgenia devoted more than 500 words to demolishing *The Picts and The Martyrs*. It was a cruel letter in which the insensitive and unimaginative Evgenia did her level best to prevent Ransome from publishing a book that she failed to understand. Yet there can be no doubt that her motives were for the best: 'My dear darling, I am very sorry I am going to hurt you very much . . . Anything is better than to have a book to your name of which you are ashamed. So cheer up!' The book was dead, the children were not being allowed to grow up and the plot involved episodes that were poor imitations of earlier books. She dismissed the wishes of those children who had written to say that when they had finished a book they felt that they wanted to read another just like it, simply because the book did not appeal to HER. The children were not having new adventures at all but were responding to troubles between adults, and these adults made the book 'too grown up and facetious'. After *Missee Lee* even

Ransome's most faithful readers would find it dull. In her 500 words Evgenia could not find a single good one to say about the story on which her husband had worked long and hard for seven months. It obviously did not occur to her that her taste might differ from that of Ransome's young British and American readers.

Jonathan Cape had put aside paper for 25 000 copies of *The Picts and The Martyrs* and there was 'consternation and monkeyhouse' in the office when Ransome read the letter and stopped publication on the spot. Looking back on the occasion, Ransome felt that he had taken the news better than any of them. He felt that part of the trouble had been that there was nobody to listen to extracts as he developed the story, and he wished that he had not turned down Margaret Renold's invitation to go and stay with her and go through the book before it was too late, because he knew how busy she was at that time.

For a time Ransome told himself that Evgenia was right and Howard wrong, and with the subject becoming taboo at home, he turned his attention to other possible projects. Cape wanted an autobiography omitting the problems of his first marriage. He thought there would always be a market for Russian stories and perhaps he could set something in the Baltic. There was a vague idea that he called 'The Death and Glories' and another entitled 'The Monotonous Brigand'. In November he began to make some progress with a tale that he called 'The River Comes First'. By then he had begun to have second thoughts about *The Picts and The Martyrs* and he secretly took a copy to his mother when he visited her in Kew. She gave a positive verdict, and on the strength of her good opinion Ransome made a small adjustment removing detail about the preparation for the burglary, and sent the manuscript to Cape. 'God bless his mother!' the cry went round the Cape offices. He added a sub-title 'or Not Welcome at All', meaning the Great Aunt. Or did it also refer to Evgenia's dislike of the book and her reception of it?

The illustrations show an increasing confidence and maturity. Unlike *Pigeon Post*, stone walls really do look like Lakeland walls — particularly in depictions of The Dogs' Home. Only 28 preliminary sketches seem to have been made, and most of these are in a tiny pocketbook. Not surprisingly, since his house was almost entirely surrounded by trees, he has caught the bosky Lake

There are still times when Windermere, for all its commercialism, can be supremely beautiful.

Windermere on a windless autumn morning looking towards the head of the lake.

The northern basin of Windermere seen from the Biskey House viewpoint above the village of Bowness.

District scenery better than ever. If as a set they are slightly inferior to those of *The Big Six*, there are several delightful evocations of his beloved lake country — 'It hasn't tumbled down yet', 'Feeling for a trout', 'At the Beckfoot gate' and 'Moving house'. The final picture, 'The Great Aunt steps ashore' is Ransome's most ambitious group of figures. Not only are Dick and Dorothea, the Great Aunt and Colonel Jolys placed centre stage, as it were, but among the surrounding crowd it is possible to identify, Nancy, Peggy, Cook, Timothy, the police sergeant and Jacky.

Cape had 22,750 copies printed by the time of publication on June 28th 1943. A return to the Alden Press and Bain & Co. resulted in a return to the appearance of *The Big Six* and earlier volumes, although they were unable to match the pre-war quality of the paper.

Ransome must have been much cheered by the glowing reviews that greeted the delayed publication. An anonymous writer in *John O' London's Weekly* caught the book's charm, saying:

*Happy are the children who know the familiar children in Arthur Ransome's books with their passion for doing things, sailing boats, building houses and cooking meals. Happy are the grown-ups who have children with whom they can share these best of children's books. Perhaps happier still are the grown-ups who can just enjoy them. All of them, anyway, will enjoy* The Picts and The Martyrs.

This view was shared by the *Manchester Guardian's* reviewer:

*Mr Ransome's gift for story-telling is rare in that the adventures of his characters provide as much fun for grown-up readers as for children, and that guarantees that for children they are first-class.*

Mary Treadgold spoke for many, when she wrote:

*After the wild doings in the far China seas with* Missee Lee *last Christmas twelvemonth, I was glad to be back in the smaller preoccupations of Beckfoot, with Nancy and Peggy Blackett entertaining the two D's in the absence of their mother. 'He that cannot contract the sight of his mind as well as disperse and dilate it wanteth a great faculty,' said Bacon. For ingenuity of plot-development on a small scale, for the raising of a Kanchenjunga of complications infinitesimal in importance to all but the few involved,* The Picts and the Martyrs *easily passes the post first among the Ransomes. . . As usual I finished, loving to the last page that perpetual expectancy of adventure in all those Ransome children — whether it is Nancy's young eager grasping of the moment, the more cautious assessment arid acceptance of events by the two D's, or the unmoved, unsurprised acquiescent detachment of the country child, Jacky — a new and endearing character.*

The review by Janet Adam-Smith in the Spectator pondered whether the Swallows books appealed to working class children or those who lived in towns. There was an unexpected sequel, for a school librarian in Shrewsbury wrote to the journal to say that at her school the books were popular with all types and ages. Ransome sent a heartfelt 'thank you' letter. 'It is a great pleasure to me to know that my books are liked in such a school as yours.' 1943 was the year when he started and abandoned the historical novel that had great potential. But it was not entirely doom and gloom. Encouragement came from an unexpected quarter in a letter from the Vice-Chancellor of Durham University who wrote saying that he had just added *The Picts and the Martyrs* to his shelf. He had begun by choosing the books as gifts for his young relations, but found that once read, he did not want to part with them. 'Really a very encouraging letter,' Ransome told his mother, 'and God knows I need a bit of encouragement, if, in spite of the local veto, I am to produce any more.'

There were some pleasures to be had at The Heald. Ransome at last succeeded in catching char under sail and there was a great celebration on the day that he caught a brace of half-pounders — a good size for Coniston. He told his mother that the difficulty was to persuade *Coch-y-bonddhu* to sail slowly enough! 'Trouble comes when you hook your fish sixty or eighty yards away and have to manage sail, rudder, rod, reel and net all at the same time with only two hands and false teeth.' That year also he was elected to The Garrick Club, and late in life he called in once a week to play chess or billiards and delight in its easy-going camaraderie.

# Chapter Fourteen

# TWO THAT GOT AWAY

IN NOVEMBER 1942, when Ransome began what some have seen as one of his most interesting works, he was still wilting from Evgenia's drenching criticism of *The Picts and The Martyrs*. As long ago as 1931 he had told Ernestine Evans that he had the beginnings of an idea that would one day become his very best book but that it needed time to ferment. It had been bubbling for more than ten years when he finally started work on his historical novel of rural life.

It was a subject close to his heart, for in spite of his salad days spent in bohemian Chelsea and his return to a London flat with approaching old age, Ransome remained a countryman. At the very end of his life, the Ransomes left London and settled into their fourth isolated Lake District home, an incredibly impractical thing to do. It says so much for Evgenia that she was prepared to go north yet again and endure the Lakeland rain while she looked after her invalid husband.

One of the pleasures of living in the Lake District was being able to fish those rivers that were once fished by his father and grandfather. Ransome's favourite trout stream, the River Bela or Beela that flows into the River Kent near its mouth, was one of those rivers. When he returned to England in 1925 and visited the river, he found that Tom Stainton, the old river keeper, had known his father and his grandfather.

He began to form an idea for a book about Tom Stainton, that would pay tribute to his values and the way of life he represented. A number of country folk had found their way into the Swallows and Amazons books: Harry Bangate, Jim Woodall, Old Simon, the Billies, Cook and Billy Lewthwaite, Neddy and Mary Swainson, Mr Dixon and Silas, Slater Bob, Jacky and the three farmers' wives. His feeling for the traditional way of life is beautifully illustrated by the following passage from *Swallowdale*. In it Young Billy tells Roger that there will also be some wrestling, and he tells him about the day long ago when he wrestled for 'a belt with a bit of silver buckle on it'.

*And with that his back straightened and he swung his old arms and rubbed his hands and clapped them together and rambled away with talk that Roger could not understand at all about half-Nelsons and cross buttocks and fair throws and lost hand-grips. But Roger did not say that he did not understand. He just listened and the talk went over his head like great poetry, only leaving him the feeling that the old man who was talking was very much stirred up by something or other that happened a very long time ago.*

Ransome carefully drew up a synopsis of 31 chapters that he called 'Gamekeeper', and thought so well of it that within a few weeks he took himself down to London to see about a publisher. He visited William Collins because he thought that his own publishers were only interested in the Swallows books, for he had seen for himself how badly they had taken the disappointment of the withdrawal of *The Picts and The Martyrs*. Collins were enthusiastic, as well they might be, but Ransome called in at Bedford Square before he returned to The Heald. What made him mention the book to Jonathan Cape is not clear, but Cape knew very well that the success of *Rod and Line* would ensure that any book of Ransome's that concerned fishing could be guaranteed an enthusiastic reception. Cape suggested that the distinguished bird artist Charles Tunnicliffe (who had illustrated Henry Williamson's *Tarka the Otter*) should be commissioned to produce the illustrations.

In the first chapter of 'The River Comes First' that he called 'The Latin School', Tom 'Staunton' plays truant from the schoolroom in Canon John Williams' vicarage where he teaches half a dozen of the village boys. When the parson comes to the river after school is over for the day Tom watches him unobserved, until the Canon's line becomes caught in a tree, when he breaks cover to free it.

There follows a description of the capture of a salmon every bit as compelling as the Death and Glories' battle with the 'World's Whopper'. With the fish safely landed, the old canon cuts a cane from a tree and gives Tom five strokes for his truancy, and afterwards exclaims, 'God forgive me, but I don't think you felt a single skelp'.

'I saw another fish move down the pool,' said Tom.

Finally, with two fine salmon on the bank, Tom is given the Latin lesson that he has missed, and the two of them return to Tom's cottage to have the fish weighed.

The fifth chapter 'The Cloudburst' is written in the first person in which Tom, now an old man, recalls a day when he was 12 and his wife Jenny, a farmer's daughter, was only eight. They had been playing on an islet in the river when they find themselves marooned after the river had risen in spate following a cloudburst. The description of Tom's rescue of Jenny is vintage Ransome.

The natural order of things is disturbed when there is the danger of organised poaching on a scale that will threaten gamekeepers and local poachers alike, and Tom involves his enemy, Bob Lidgett, the son of a poacher who he knows is not above a little poaching himself, in order to try to guard the river. The three children managed to foil the gang of poachers and he and Bob become friends. Tom is clearly a bright young lad, and against his wishes he is taken to London in order to better himself by becoming an assistant in a fishing-tackle shop. He does not remain there for long before setting out to make his way back north. Arriving at last at the river he meets his friend, the old curate who prepares the way for his return home and final acceptance as his father's under-keeper.

*The gamekeeper's cottage stood where it stands today, set back in the edge of the wood and looking out over the straight bit of the river that is known as the Long Dub. Some of the trees have grown since then, but others have been cut, and probably it was then much as it is now, sheltered by the wood from the south-west wind and catching the morning sun across the river, it was a two-storied cottage, rough cast and whitewashed, with a slate-roofed porch covered with a climbing rose that had been planted on the gamekeeper's wedding day, a present to Tom's mother from the old gardener at the hall.*

By the beginning of April 1943 Ransome had pulled together his notes and was ready to start 'The River Comes First', although he was still hoping that Margaret Renold would come up with an idea for some wild yarn without any Swallows and Amazons. By the end of the month he had 49 pages and he added seven more before stopping for good a week later. Why he should have stopped at this point is not immediately apparent. The subject was one close to his heart, he had a synopsis with which he seemed satisfied, and so far as it is possible to tell, he was enjoying the writing. It is likely that he realised too that on those 49 pages he had done some of his finest work. Perhaps the answer lies in something that he wrote to Margaret Renold later that year. 'God knows I need a bit of encouragement, if, in spite of the local veto, I am to produce any more'. The reason for the veto of Ransome's 'critic on the hearth' is not difficult to guess. Ransome had told his mother to ask the family never to mention *The Picts and The Martyrs* in letters, as Evgenia was 'miserable' because he had gone against her strongest wishes — which probably meant that she was sulking and generally making home life difficult. She had never approved of the idea of 'The River Comes First' (she must have forgotten the success of *Rod and Line*)— which might explain why so many years had passed before he began to write and why he never returned to it again. At the time that he abandoned the book he believed that one day he would be able to pick it up again. The sad thing is that he never did, and all that remains is a reminder of what might have been.

For those who would like to know exactly how old Ransome thought the *Swallows and Amazons* were, there is a single sheet of paper written about this time that clears the question for good and all. In *Swallows and Amazons* (that is placed in 1930 — not 1929) John and Nancy are 12, Susan and Peggy are 11, Titty is 9 and Roger is 7. By the time of the proposed sequel to *The Picts and The Martyrs* in 1933 that he called 'Swallows & Co', John and Nancy are 15, Peggy and Susan are 14, Dorothea is 13, Titty, Dick and Joe are 12, Bill is 11 and Roger and Pete are 10.

It has not been possible to place the time exactly when Ransome turned his attention to 'The Death

A rare photograph of Banhams (Jonnatt's boatsheds) beside the staithe at Horning, probably dating from the early 1950s.

and Glories' (presumably a change of title from 'Swallows & Co'). At first it was thought that it was begun after the publication of *Great Northern?* But the pages of sketches for the book are sandwiched between those for *The Picts and The Martyrs* and *Great Northern?* Perhaps the best guess is the first half of 1944, as one of the sketches was made in April.

Ransome abandoned his first and rather unusual opening that linked the story to *The Picts and The Martyrs* after a page or so:

*There is no getting away from it. Grown-ups are at the bottom of most things that happen in the holidays, even when it seems that they have been left out of it altogether. Thus nothing in these adventures would have been quite the same if it had not been for Mrs Callum writing to Mrs*

*Barrable and telling her that Professor Callum was correcting examination papers, but using the same blue pencil with which he marked the papers to put a cross against likely boats that were offered for hire on the Broads. Mrs Barrable hurriedly wrote back to say that August was not the time to go there, and she drew a picture of Horning Reach with sailing boats packed like sardines, ramming each other, bumping each other and charging for safety into the banks while motor cruisers ploughed through them, like whales charging through a packed shoal of small fry. 'Not in August, my dear,' she wrote. 'One can hardly hear oneself speak and the place is a seething cauldron of hullabaloos. If only I knew where to go, I would clear out myself until things get quieter again.'*

And of course, Mrs Callum invited her old teacher to accompany them to the lakes. . .

The draft opens in confidant fashion a fortnight or so after the end of *The Picts and The Martyrs*. Joe, Bill and Pete are sitting on the cabin top of the *Death and Glory*. They have tied up to the posts outside Jonnatt's, the boatbuilders, because there is no room along Horning Staithe. Hired sailing boats and motor cruisers are tied up all along the staithe, from the wall of the inn garden down to Jonnatt's. There is a noisy crowd of holidaymakers going to and fro between their boats and the little shops across the green. More and more boats keep coming up, looking for a place, finding none, and bumping in to tie up to the boats already moored there. It was the second week in August and every boat-letter on the Broads has let every boat he had.

'Good thing birds don't nest in August,' Bill had said once at a meeting of the Coot Club in the shed by Dr Dudgeon's house. 'Did, they wouldn't have a chance.'

The Death and Glories have become disillusioned with salvage since so many visitors are too mean to produce a tip after being rescued by a neat piece of salvage work. Half of Horning seems to be away on holiday when a postcard from the D's at the lake in the north and a chance word from Mrs Barrable about Jonnatt's newly-built cruiser that is about to be sent by road to that very lake, sets Joe thinking . . .

The Coots watch the delicate job of manoeuvring the cruiser onto the trailer for its 'voyage by road'. They decide to take the *Death and Glory* down river and put her safely in the Wilderness dyke, planning to return at dusk to see the cruiser depart with Pete's father who is to travel with the lorry driver so that he can deliver the cruiser to her owner. Joe leads the way aboard the cruiser while nobody is looking, and almost before Bill and Pete have time to think, they find that they have stowed away and are driving through the night.

At this point there is a pause in the typescript, and the various notes indicate that Ransome considered possible developments once the cruiser has passed Norwich and is fairly on its way. In one the boys are discovered when the lorry stops at an all-night café. Pete's father wants them to remain there until the lorry returns, but the driver points out that the boys could be useful during the cruiser's trial trip. In another note, having arrived at the boatbuilders in Rio Bay, the boys meet the D's who have brought *Scarab* in for repair after Professor Callum has damaged the rudder. After such an exciting departure, the arrival is a disappointment and Ransome abandoned that idea.

Then Ransome wrote a short chapter 'It's Gone!' after the lorry has driven off shortly before they arrive in Rio without the stowaways but with Joe's white rat still aboard the cruiser. The Death and Glories find their way to the lake and after hunting around the boatyards and failing to find the lorry, discover that the cruiser is already afloat and moored to a landing stage. Peeping through the windows Joe spots the owner feeding the white rat.

The narrative stops at that point but it seems that the owner befriends the boys, for in the next chapter 'One Way of Meeting Nancy' he takes them down the lake the following day to look for Dixon's Farm. They have just transferred from the cruiser to a rowing boat so that they can reach Dixon's Farm landing where they believe the D's are staying. They see three small dinghies, one of which capsizes and there are bodies in the water. "Salvage!' cries Joe, and the salvage company hurry to the rescue.

'Shiver my timbers!" said an angry voice as Joe grabs her, 'What are you playing at? Tearing my hair out by the roots. Hullo! Did I get your nose? Good.'

There aare further notes and fragments that tell of some of the possibilities that occurred to him once the Death and Glories have met up with the Swallows and Amazons — Nancy says that the Coots must stay — telegram to Mrs Barrable. . . Inspired by his own success as a char fisherman he thought of a fleet of sailing boats like tunny-fishers each flying a flag for every fish caught — the cruiser should thread its way through the story — Professor Callum and his wife must be taught to sail — the question of how the Coots are to return hangs over them all — the houseboat, having become the parent ship of the fishing fleet, leaves her moorings in a gale, while Captain Flint and Timothy are up on High Topps. The helpless vessel is in danger of being driven ashore and it is Joe who leads the salvage operation. When it is time for them to return, Captain Flint insists on paying for their tickets and adds something by way of pocket money.

'Geewhizz!' says Joe as the train pulls out. 'Salvage ain't so bad after all.'

The story of the Death and Glories stowaway voyage by road has echoes of Hull and Whitlock's *Escape to Persia* in which the first eight chapters are devoted to the Hunterley's clandestine journey from London to Exmoor. Ransome must have seen the possibilities of unusual journeys at that time for there is also a hint of Tom Staunton's adventures on the Great North Road.

In earlier books Ransome had successfully used the visitors' point of view — the Walkers in *Swallows and Amazons* and *Swallowdale*, the D's in *Winter Holiday* and *Coot Club* and the Swallows and Amazons in *Secret Water*, and it would have been fascinating to meet the Swallows and Amazons and the lake country through the eyes of Joe, Bill and Pete. Ransome recognised only too well that in spite of its possibilities, his story lacked a backbone. He had passed similar judgements in the past, but this time there would be no solution. Instead, he turned to the less demanding task of fleshing out somebody else's plot.

It is worth every effort to obtain a copy of *Coots in the North and other stories* that was introduced and gently edited by Hugh Brogan and first published in 1988, for the book contains a total of 70 pages of 'The River Comes First' and 'Coots in the North' — and, as Brogan says, 'nobody fully knows Joe, Bill and Pete who has not set out with them on their adventures to the north'.

Raising the cruiser *Bonnka* (Norfolk for a buxom young lady) in Jonnatt's shed. Sketch for 'The Death and Glories'.

# Chapter Fifteen

# GREAT NORTHERN?

FOR RANSOME'S FINAL BOOK about the Swallows and Amazons, he turned at last to someone else's plot. For the previous dozen years or so he had requested plots from all manner of people, yet useful as a few of the suggestions had been, the main thrust of each plot had remained his own. The possible exception is *Pigeon Post* about which so little is known, it is quite possible that Oscar Gnosspelius suggested the gold-copper confusion as well as supplying all the necessary details about mining.

Although there is no record of pages of *Coots in the North* that Ransome completed during the summer of 1944, he seems to have reached the stage of trying to decide what the great cast of Swallows, Amazons, D's, Death and Glories, Captain Flint, Timothy and Professor Callum and his wife could get up to after the arrival of the Coots.

Around that time there was also the very appealing possibility of a book of fishing flies written in collaboration with Charles Renold. Cape would have been happy to produce such a book, but the difficulties of colour reproduction could not be overcome and the project was abandoned. So, when a long letter with a complete synopsis arrived, Ransome was ready to seriously consider any plot that might look as if it would present fewer problems than 'The Death and Glories'. His correspondent was Major Myles North, a District Commisioner in the Colonial Service in East Africa. North's family lived in the Lake District and his parents had known the Ransomes. He was a serious ornithologist who had specialised in

making recordings of African bird song and he had been considering what bird could play a part in the further adventures of The Swallows, Amazons and D's.

North came up with a plot that possessed the great virtue of being thoroughly plausible. During the 1940s, some Great Northern Divers were known to spend all year around our shores. In the standard reference book of the time — the five volume *Handbook of British Birds* — the bird is said to have been known to spend the summer in the Outer Hebrides and Shetland and was thought to have nested in Shetland, although this had never been proved. The first recorded nesting divers were found in Wester Ross in 1970, and today it is thought that between 2,500 and 3,000 birds can be found wintering in British waters.

In North's synopsis the *Wild Cat* with its crew of Captain Flint and the Ss, As & D's, is cruising among the Outer Hebrides in early August when Dick discovers that what he thought were nesting Black-throated Divers were in fact Great Northerns. A rather unlikely development is the discovery that when the egg-collector's yacht appears, it is crewed by Peter Duck and Bill. In the first synopsis, North suggested that the egg collector himself was a figure of fun with his cap, plus-fours and protruding teeth. North felt there needed to be a postscript at the end of the book, after the eggs have been returned to the nest and he suggested five possibilities. Ransome's reaction to all this was to cover the manuscript with ticks and 'no's, but it is clear that on reflection he changed his mind over a number of the over-hasty 'no's.

He replied explaining the difference between *Peter Duck, Missee Lee* (which North does not appear to have read) and the other books, so that it would not be possible for Bill and Peter Duck to appear in this one.

In North's synopsis there is no 'Young Chieftain' whose introduction was Ransome's major change to North's plot, but his other revision has led some readers to class *Great Northern?* with the two romances *Peter Duck* and *Missee Lee*. Ransome's concern over the motivation of the laird caused him to change the time of the year so that the laird would think that the trespassing strangers wandering over his hills were a threat to his herd of deer, frightening the hinds off his land just before they are due to give birth. Although it would be quite possible for Dick to have spotted a pair of

In *Great Northern?* Scrubbers Bay was situated alongside another bay where the *Pterodactyl* anchored. Opinions differ, but these striking little coves are to be found in the right place on the east coast of the Isle of Lewis.

late-nesting Great Northerns in August, the voyaging of the *Sea Bear* could not be placed later than the month of June or the hinds would have already given birth. Even so, he was not comfortable with having to put the voyage into term time: 'June would be best. Why they are not at school, heaven only knows!!!!!'

Ransome began *Great Northern?* at the end of August 1944 and by November he had completed 173 pages. It was at this point that he decided to introduce the young McGinty who would discover and then spy on the invaders. It was necessary to create a fictitious landscape, with elements drawn together from various parts of the Isle of Lewis, although the careful reader will soon spot that the

harbour is Stornoway and 'the Head' is Tiumpan Head. Scrubbers' Cove is somewhere in the area of the two tiny coves marked Port Bun a'Ghlinne north-west of Tiumpan Head.

In December Ransome's mother died. They had corresponded regularly throughout his life and because she was a sympathetic and intelligent audience, these letters allowed him to relieve some of his inner tensions, not least with Evgenia. Although she had been against his early scribbles, she had been financially supportive during the difficult times and an ever-ready help with the illustrations, as well as being an exemplary proofreader.

By the end of the year he had reached 280 pages that he thought was 'awful dull stuff' but he consoled himself with the thought that it would not matter too much if he should have to do a lot of rewriting after visiting the Hebrides to check the details.

In January he only managed 18 pages and announced that he was now too old for stories. He was soon himself again, and dismissing North's suggestion of making the Egg Collector a more sympathetic character, for in that case, as he pointed out, he would be bound to get pally with Captain Flint. In the middle of February he stopped altogether with only a further eight pages added.

Life at The Heald had completely lost its charm. Evgenia had already declared that she would sell as soon as the war was over, and Ransome would have liked to move to London where they had the opportunity to buy Rupert Hart-Davis's Highgate house, but Evgenia would not consider it because the garden was too big.

Ransome's correspondence with North had an unexpected bonus when he sent North a drawing of a feather that was needed in order to make a particular salmon fly. North recognised the drawing as a feather from the neck of a Vulturine Guineafowl and promptly despatched a preserved head and neck.

In March 1945 they made their plans to leave The Heald, on June 1st and put their furniture into store in Manchester while they spent six weeks in a hotel at Loweswater. Before the move they visited Stornoway on Lewis so that Ransome could collect local colour.

They left Loweswater in the middle of July and drove over 300 miles to London arriving at 9.30 in the evening. Jonathan Cape loaned them his flat while they found themselves a permanent home. At first they made a round of possible areas in East Anglia, visiting Ipswich, Felixstowe, Woodbridge, Horning and Oulton Broad, where they visited *Selina King* in her shed. Regretfully, they decided that the boat was now too large for Ransome to handle, and they called in at Pin Mill to see Harry King who said that he would be able to build him a new boat with wood stored from before the war.

None of the places that they visited on their travels appealed to Evgenia, and they returned to London, and ended up renting a flat in Weymouth Street, within comfortable walking distance of the Garrick Club. Evgenia soon began to have the place knocked about, and on one occasion Ransome found himself sleeping in the bathroom! Once the transformation was complete, Evgenia announced that she regretted the move and was tired of the place already.

There were some advantages to living in London however, and Ransome was able to visit the BBC and discuss the new adaptation of *Swallows and Amazons* with the head of Children's Hour, Derek McCulloch, and on a memorable Saturday afternoon he visited Twickenham in the company of Rupert Hart-Davis and saw England narrowly defeat Scotland in a 'splendid game'.

Against this background of upheaval in the home and the noisy wireless in the neighbouring flat it is surprising that Ransome had progressed so far with *Great Northern?* that by February 1946 he had a draft for Wren Howard to read. Howard confirmed that the start was dull and he suggested more dialogue, and added that he thought that more should be made of the mysterious Gaels. Ransome found all this very helpful as it only confirmed what he suspected, and was cheered when Howard encouraged him to keep going, and he resolved to introduce the Gaels earlier.

In April he decided that the chapter where John and Nancy act as red herrings was not working and that he could introduce more fun if they were shadowed by one of the sailors from the *Pterodactyl*.

In the New Year he pressed ahead, reassured by the news that sales in 1945 had reached the 50 000 mark! In May he read through all the 407 pages and decided that, after all, it would be a mistake to continue. The book appears to have been saved by Evgenia, for a week later, he noted in his diary that she thought that it would be all right to go ahead with the book.

They visited the Hebrides again in June, and stayed on the Atlantic coast of Lewis in a fishing lodge near Uig. The lodge came in useful as the model for the stronghold of the Gaels and the neighbouring countryside provided the country of the red herrings, although the origin of the cove where the *Sea Bear* is scrubbed remains a subject for debate.

There was an element of farce about the ongoing saga of their new boat. Ransome had mis-read the plans and was surprised to find that there was not enough headroom over the bunks, for which he blamed the boat's designer, Laurent

Giles. *Peter Duck* was eventually launched with Evgenia very much against having any sort of boat. At the beginning of October they had a trial trip and promptly sold *Peter Duck* to the designer and his partner. A month later they bought it back at a loss of £300.

In November Ransome wrote a fourth version of the opening chapter — and this time Evgenia let it pass. By the end of the year, he could do no more with *Great Northern?* and after thinking about it for a few days, he delivered the typescript to Wren Howard's office shortly after New Year 1947.

*Great Northern?* was as fully illustrated as its predecessors, and if the Isle of Lewis landscape is not captured with the same feeling as his Lake District and East Anglian pictures it is hardly surprising, considering how intimately Ransome knew these places. There was a last-minute panic at the printers when Ransome redrew the picture of the *Pterodactyl's* cabin at the last minute in order to lower the roof and show prototypically correct fore-and-aft roof planking. What Ransome failed to notice was that Peggy had crept into the picture 'Dick Goes off to the Lochs' in place of Dorothea, and many copies had been sold before he could correct it.

An incredible 44,500 copies of *Great Northern?* were printed before publication the following August. It had been four years since *The Picts and The Martyrs* had appeared and *Great Northern?* had a warm welcome. A note at the beginning of the book explains that the identity of the loch where the divers were nesting had been deliberately obscured, and inquisitive readers were warned off with the threat that if they started detective work they would make enemies of the crew of the *Sea Bear*. The essential part played by Myles North was recognised in the book's dedication as the person 'who, knowing a good deal of what happened, asked me to write the full story'.

The final picture, 'Farewell to the *Sea Bear*', showing the young McGinty watching, through binoculars as the *Sea Bear* heads out to sea, illustrates nothing in the text, and was perhaps unconsciously prophetic.

And so, Ransome brought his remarkable achievement to a close at the age of 63. He had devoted almost twenty years to the creation of the Swallows and Amazons canon and had written and revised around a million words in the process. He had flirted with the idea of 'Swallows in Syria' to please the Altounyan children and 'The Nandi Cub', a Kenyan tale to please Myles North, but these had never progressed beyond a few rough notes. In 1948 the Ransomes moved back to the Lake District — yet another unfortunate move — to a large eighteenth century manor house and for a few months he enjoyed being 'Lord of the Manor'. The pleasure was short-lived as the place was too much for them and they headed for London once more.

Sales of the Swallows and Amazons books had topped the million mark and Ransome occupied himself with his autobiography that he insisted should not be published until after his death. He once confided that he still had ideas for some Swallows books that would have their place in the series. He was hardly serious, but it is interesting that he realised that *Great Northern?* should not be followed, although he might have squeezed more adventures into earlier holidays. There are those who think that the series had rightly ended with *The Picts and The Martyrs* and the promise of an eternal five weeks of holiday still to come.

Ransome was granted the sort of retirement that his readers would have wished. He continued to sail into his 71st year, when he made his second Channel crossing at the helm. His final home was once more in the Lake District, and in spite of increasing infirmity, he continued to fish until he was 76 when he made his final catch — a fine 7lb salmon.

Finally, he received the public recognition that he deserved, being made an Honorary Litt. D. from his father's old university in Leeds and an Honorary M.A. from Durham. He was awarded the C.B.E. shortly before his 70th birthday. He died at the age of 83, and he and Evgenia are buried in a tiny churchyard in the beautiful and peaceful Rusland Valley, midway between Windermere and Coniston.

Uig Bay on the Atlantic Coast of Lewis where Arthur Ransome
spent a holiday while collecting local colour for *Great Northern?*

The fishing fleet in Stornoway harbour with the modern counterparts of the high-bowed fishing boats with their short stumpy masts and wheelhouses that were seen by the crew of the *Sea Bear*.

Uig Gorge, with Uig Lodge (the Castle of the Gaels) where Arthur Ransome stayed, on the skyline.

Another view of the twin coves at Port Bun a' Ghlinne that might
have inspired Scrubbers' Bay. (courtesy David Allcock)

# AFTERWORD

IT IS EIGHTY YEARS since the four Walker children set sail in a borrowed 13ft dinghy in search of adventure in *Swallows and Amazons*, and as several writers have observed, changed the course of children's literature. At that time the world of children's books was dominated by school stories and tales of exotic adventure aimed at either boys or girls. There was a great deal of 'hack' writing that satisfied the demand for 'reward books' intended to be given as presents, and printed on thick, poor quality paper. Ransome deplored these 'imitation books', and pointed out that children would never learn to recognize poor books until they had met good ones. He always believed that there were too many books for children being published and he hated 'the dreadful idea that newness is a virtue in itself so that books are meant to be read only once'.

The reason that books had meant so much to him as a small boy, he said, was because he did not have too many of them, so that those that he had, were reread until he almost knew them off by heart. 'A good book is not merely a thing that keeps a child (or a grown-up person) amused while reading. It is an experience he shares, it peoples his world and lets him share in other lives, enriches by exercising his own power of imaginary living and so enriches life itself.'

More, even than that, there are those whose lives have been shaped by reading the Swallows and Amazons books. The circumnavigators Calare Francis and Dame Ellen MacArthur were inspired to take up sailing and David Bellamy developed his life-long passion for natural history from having read the books when they were young.

Almost from the time that he quit his study of chemistry at the Yorkshire College, Ransome wanted to write for children. His earliest attempts written in the style of the little nature books of that time sufficiently impressed the Collingwoods that they encouraged his tentative steps towards becoming a children's writer.

Ransome would not have been able to give the Altounyans the very special gift that he wished to make within the existing genres of children's books, nor could it have sprung from his childhood holidays at Nibthwaite. Perhaps the closest antecedent was *Bevis, the Story of a Boy* in which Richard Jeffries looked back towards his own childhood exploits in the country.

It is a strange child indeed, who does not look forward to the school holidays in which there is time and space for adventures — at least in books — and in the Swallows and Amazons books, readers become intimates of an engaging group of children having believable adventures in real places. Since the Second World War, the books have also allowed readers to return to a simpler and less troubled age. As Sylvia Lynd put it, 'the life we live with Mr Ransome is simply irresistible.'

Ransome always asserted that he never wrote for children in particular, and when Helen Ferris asked him for some help as she was due to speak on the difference between writing for adults and writing for boys and girls, he replied that he really could not tell her because he knew 'absolutely nothing about it'. He could not imagine how to write for a particular audience, child or adult, since that would mean changing the original focus of the book with the result that it could never be any good. Writing FOR children could only result in written-down affairs that would reflect the enormous gap between writer and readers. He explained that he never thought of his audience, but wrote about those things that he found good fun.

During the war when his protégé Pamela Whitlock was uncertain of the public for whom she wanted to write, Ransome was adamant; 'Good books are not written FOR anyone. They are OVERHEARD ... You are the only public that you ought to consider'. He said much the same thing on several occasions. 'I believe that no matter who reads it, a good book is always one written by the author for himself. . . *Alice* is a good book, not because the story was first invented 'for' a young Miss Liddell, but because Lewis Carroll got a great deal of private fun out of writing it for himself.' In one of his weekly articles for the *Manchester Guardian* he had written, 'Words, as far as possible, should be heard and not seen. In all good writing they are heard by the author before he made them visible by writing them down, which he did solely for convenience and with the object of letting other people hear them.' He liked to quote Stevenson on *Treasure Island*: 'It's awful fun, boys stories. You just indulge the pleasure of your heart; no trouble, no strain'. Ransome's tragedy was that his fun was forever laced with self-doubt. Because of his self-doubt and the effect of the unsparing verdicts of the 'critic on the hearth' there were times when there was more strain than he could bear. Yet it was only when he told himself a story that had satisfied both the boy and the master craftsman within that his work touched greatness.

Ransome himself remained modest about his achievement, 'If by good fortune, children enjoy what you enjoy, why then you are a writer of children's books. . . No special credit to you, but simply thumping good luck.'

What is Arthur Ransome's secret? Above all is his genius as a master storyteller. He excels in the art of narration as few writers for children have. Will the D's, on their sledge rushing over the ice reach the North Pole? Will the Farland twins aboard the wherry ever catch the Teasel? Throughout the series he effortlessly compels the reader to ask the question, 'What happens next?' Who could resist to urge to read on after coming to 'Softly, at first, as if it hardly meant it, the snow began to fall,' from *Winter Holiday* or 'A smell of new-mown hay drifted from the meadows on the further side of the river "There isn't a lovelier place in all the world," thought Dorothea. London last night, and now Beckfoot. The summer holidays had begun,' from *The Picts and The Martyrs*?

Ransome wrote about those things that he was enthusiastic about, that he had experienced himself and the things for which he cared. He *had* camped on Wild Cat Island, climbed Kanchenjunga and raced dinghies on Coniston and Windermere. He *had* skated on frozen Windermere and watched the Dragon Festival in Hankow. He *had* sailed across the North Sea to Holland and cruised on the Broads in a yacht similar to the *Teasel*.

He cared passionately about the fictional children of his heart — particularly the younger ones — the D's, Titty and Roger and the Death and Glories all of whom became very real to him. During the years at Broke Farm his teenage friends Josephine Russell and Jill Busk were used to hearing Ransome bringing Dick and Dorothea into everyday conversation as if they really existed.

Readers have reread their favourite Ransomes throughout their lives because of the great attraction of its characters. No two are alike, for Ransome created his leading players so exactly that young readers were ready to believe that they were real. Perhaps his favourites were the two clever little girls — Titty the conjurer of romance who can transform the most ordinary event with her imagination and gentle Dorothea happily living in two worlds, asking no more than to be accepted by the Swallows and Amazons. Dorothea's brother Dick, the myopic single-minded young scientist is a triumph of characterisation, for he could so easily have become a stereotypical swot. Roger, being the youngest is responsible for much of the humour and many of the lighter moments, yet he has an independent streak that is neatly summed up by Dorothea when she remarks that he could never have been turned into a Pict. Nancy Blackett is a joyous creation. Impulsive, irrepressible and at times unsettling, she is also generous and kind.

Of course there have been those who have commented unfavourably that Ransome's characters are middle-class. One reviewer wondered if the books were only read by families who could afford cooks, nannies and private boathouses. At this Ransome observed that holidays spent on a working farm cost less than a holiday in Blackpool and he speculated, tongue in cheek, if the reviewer thought that only those of the 'blood royal' could enjoy Hamlet?

As Fred Inglis points out in *The Pursuit of Happiness* that, 'the greatness of Arthur Ransome's best novels has very little to do with the children in them being at a private school and possessing . . . spare cash'.

There is a certain timelessness about the five books set in Ransome's Lakeland Arcadia, heavily influenced as they were by his own childhood holidays at Coniston. It is also classless. In *The Picts and The Martyrs*, Dorothea asks who are the old couple at Swainson's Farm? Nancy answers simply, 'Friends'. And so they are. When Ransome received the text of Hugh Shelley's monograph he was privately scathing, calling it a 'more or less illiterate pamphlet' but the only suggestion that he made was to request a footnote stating that there were no 'lower orders' in the Lake Country.

One of the delights of the Lake District and Broads books is Ransome's keen ear for dialect.

This was challenged in 1953, and Ransome replied robustly, "'Folk generally what do." —This is exactly as it should be. It is good Lake Country speech, and the speaker would have choked if he had been asked to say it otherwise.'

Another charge laid against his writing is that at times it becomes too technical. There was a suggestion when *We Didn't Mean to Go to Sea* was being translated into Swedish that some of the technical detail should be removed. Ransome would have none of it, believing that children were prepared to accept and would enjoy the descriptions of such things as the art of sailing, 'I do not believe that there exists a Swedish child who does not know enough about a boat to want to know more, and the whole point of my books is that they do not insult children by assuming that they do not want to use their brains or have no brains to use.'

Ransome expected his readers to take their reading seriously. He was writing at a time when reading had a prominent place on the timetable and was well taught. It was a time without television, when radio was in its infancy and when parents read to their children. Looking back to his own childhood, Ransome said that he had more reason to be grateful to his mother's habit of reading than anything else. He saw no need to limit his vocabulary or modify his style, as another adult writer turned children's author, C.S. Lewis did when he began writing the 'Narnia' series in the 1950s.

There may be some justification for the charge of too much technical detail but Ransome's sheer boyish enthusiasm for descriptions of how things are done produced some of his best writing. Whether he is detailing the drawn out battle with the 'World's Whopper' or explaining how John fastened the square and triangle signals in *Winter Holiday* he is having fun and such fun is infectious.

A more serious charge appears to be the one that Ransome never allows his children to develop naturally. Certainly, the childless Evgenia condemned *The Picts and The Martyrs* for that reason — among others. It is unlikely that the readers that Ransome was pleased to allow to 'overhear' his stories would have been in the least bothered if John and Nancy and the others did not seem to 'grow up'. According to Malcolm Saville, whose writing career began during the Second World War, his readers made it clear that they did

not want the Lone Piners to grow up, and for at least twelve books the members of The Lone Pine Club continued to have adventures at the same age.

Having said that, the Swallows and Amazons do grow older, perhaps more through their experiences or force of circumstances than chronological age alone. In *We Didn't Mean to Go to Sea*, the John and Susan of *Swallows and Amazons* could never have brought the *Goblin* safely to Holland, and both grow significantly during their passage across the North Sea. The Nancy who put a firework on the roof of her uncle's houseboat would not have suppressed her natural inclinations in *The Picts and The Martyrs* in order to successfully arrange things so that her friends had the holiday that her mother had promised and her unwelcome guest found nothing about which she could complain. Nor would she have intervened to save the G.A. from possible embarrassment at the hands of the police. The Dorothea of *Coot Club* would not have led the five detectives as she did in *The Big Six*.

Perhaps the character who changes the most is Roger; who is clearly the youngest and is content to follow others in *Swallows and Amazons* and *Swallowdale*. He has become mischievous by the time of *Winter Holiday* and more so in *Pigeon Post*, reverting to the eager follower of his elder brother when real danger threatens in *We Didn't Mean to Go to Sea*. The presence of Bridget in *Secret Water* brings out his more responsible side but by *Great Northern?* Roger has become an outsider, scornful of the others at times and not particularly likable, until he becomes a loyal Sea Bear once more, when he sees the egg collector, and realises that only swift action can save the divers.

Of course, Ransome himself remained a child, as the young Lola Kinel was quick to realise, and even in old age it was said of him that his company was like that of a very knowledgeable schoolboy. Throughout his life he maintained the enthusiasms of a child. During his days at Low Ludderburn he would drop in from time to time at Barkbooth and would join in with great gusto into whatever the young Desmond and Dick Kelsall were playing. Everything from his new plot to the eccentricities of the engine of his yacht was either 'gorgeous' or 'frightful'.

One of the reasons that Ransome struggled with the development of his plots was his determination that they should move forward by his characters responding to events by being themselves.

As a professional writer, Ransome took careful note of his readership, whilst paying them the compliment of giving them those things that pleased him. It was essential, he said, to have a child within a year or two in age of each intended reader if they were to identify with the characters in the story. Once the series was established and for the rest of his life, he received many fan letters. These he answered courteously by hand on his decorated postcard. He sketched out the following scene that was supposed to have taken place in the cabin of the houseboat about four years after the publication of *Swallows and Amazons*.

*Nancy is flicking through a great pile of letters on the cabin table. Susan is busy at the stove. John is showing Roger how to make an eye-splice at the end of a rope. Titty is writing home. Peggy is looking out of a porthole.*

'Do we do anything about this lot?' asked Nancy. 'He keeps on asking what to say.'

'Couldn't he just put the letters in the fire?' said John.

'Lots of them send stamped addressed envelopes,' answered Nancy. 'He says he's got to answer them.'

'I don't see why,' said Roger. 'Nobody asked them to write.'

'But there's the stamped envelopes,' said Peggy.

'He could steam off the stamps and use them for writing to us when we're at school,' said Roger.

'He wouldn't do that anyway!'

'It's the things they ask,' said Nancy. 'Everyone asks "Are they real?"'

'Beastly cheek!' said Roger.

'If I had time, I'd see about who's real!' said Nancy.

'And what about the ones who ask him to tell the real names of our best places?' said Peggy.

'He's said too much already,' said Nancy. 'Look at the way they found out the harbour on Wild Cat Island in spite of his careful moving around of geography.'

' It's awful finding someone had been at our old harbour and painted the leading mark with white paint. They must have read the book.'

'We'll begin to think he ought never to have written the books. Anyway I know that he must have let out too much'.

The young authors of The Far-distant Oxus trilogy had a similar problem with their readers wanting to know more about the enigmatic and mysterious Maurice. The truth was that the authors knew did not know themselves.

Perhaps it is fitting to end with an appreciative young fan. The following is said to be a genuine conversation between a Learned Professor and his Daughter, following a visit to *Twelfth Night* and it appeared in Jonathan Cape's house journal, *Now and Then*:

D.  I hope there's another one soon. I like Shakespeare.

L.P.  Some people think he was the greatest writer that ever lived.

D.  Yes, I think so too — except, perhaps Arthur Ransome.

L.P.  I don't think Arthur Ransome's as good as Shakespeare.

D.  (with great derision)  You only say that because he isn't dead yet!

# ACKNOWLEDGEMENTS

It was David Joy who gave me the chance twenty-five years ago to share my enthusiasm for Arthur Ransome when Dalesman Books agreed to publish my picture book, *Arthur Ransome's Lakeland*. Ten years ago David published *Arthur Ransome and the world of the Swallows and Amazons* under the imprint of Great Northern Books. When he asked me last year if I would like to have a go at another book about the favourite children's author who has become an iconic figure, it was with particular pleasure that I welcomed the opportunity to renew our partnership, and I suggested a 'sort of literary biography'. It was David who thought that it should be illustrated with the best of the thousands of Swallows and Amazons-related photographs that I had taken over the years, the selection of which was a very pleasurable but difficult task.

Like all who have followed, I have been inspired by the pioneering work of Hugh Brogan and Christina Hardyment, whose books appeared a couple of years before *Arthur Ransome's Lakeland*.

As always, I am most appreciative of the support of the Arthur Ransome Literary Estate and permission to reproduce his work. Similarly, I am pleased to acknowledge permission from The Random House Group Ltd to reproduce extracts from the Swallows and Amazons books and also from the correspondence in the Jonathan Cape archive at Reading University.

The Abbot Hall Museum of Lakeland Life and Industry in Kendal has provided much invaluable information from their Arthur Ransome collection. I am grateful to several at the museum over the years, from Mary Birkett, OBE in the early days to James Arnold at the present, who has kindly allowed me to reproduce images from Arthur Ransome's sketchbooks. The other major archive is held by the Special Collections in the Brotherton Library at the University of Leeds where Ann Farr has been immensely helpful over the years. For this work, I acknowledge permission to reproduce the two photographs from their large collection of Arthur Ransome's snapshots. My thanks also go to the Society of Authors for permission to reproduce the letter from John Masefield. I would also like to thank those who supplied photographs for reproduction.

It was a privilege and a pleasure to know Taqui Altounyan and her sister Brigit and to have met Susie, Titty and Roger — the unsuspecting recipients of Arthur Ransome's very special gift of *Swallows and Amazons*.

Writing a book of this kind is by no means a solitary occupation; rather it is the result of collaboration between the author and a host of friends and acquaintances. For example, the transcriptions of Arthur Ransome's diaries made some years ago by John Berry and Ted Alexander have been a continuous source of information. Though the actual writing has occupied but a few months, the work of researching and recording has occupied a much longer period and I could claim that it had its beginnings when I wrote a 'fan' letter to Arthur Ransome more than fifty years ago.

In the preparation of this book I have been cheered on my way by Claire Barnett from the USA, who has fulfilled the role of both 'Margaret Renold' and a kindly 'Evgenia'.

The starting point for *Arthur Ransome: Master Storyteller* was *The Best of Childhood* that was produced by Amazon Publications for members of The Arthur Ransome Society in 2004, and I am pleased to acknowledge the part played by the other members of the group: Paul Crisp, Claire Kendal-Price, Trevor Johnston, David Jones and Diana Sparkes.

Finally, my thanks once more to my editor at Great Northern Books, David Joy who also made the final selection of the illustrations, and to the designer David Burrill who has produced some stunning pages and a wonderful jacket.

Arthur Ransome's reply to the
author's fan letter that
prompted a lifelong search for
the secret places in the books.

## HERRIOT – A Vet's Life
### W. R. Mitchell

*The real story of Alf Wight*

Bill Mitchell was recently voted the Dales National Park's greatest living cultural icon. Polling was a feature of each National Park to mark their 60th anniversary. In the Dales, Alf Wight – much better known as James Herriot, a celebrated vet, won the main accolade as an icon who had died but was still revered.

In this book, the two are re-united, with Bill Mitchell as the author and Alf as the main character, along with his son Jim, a vet who often accompanied him on his rounds. Both applied their veterinary skills to ailing farmstock and household pets in the Pennine dales and across the North East Moors.

The text looks back at the memorable era that saw the books of James Herriot rise from obscurity to worldwide best-seller status, with the films All Creatures Great and Small and It Shouldn't Happen to a Vet preceding the incredibly popular TV series in the 1970s and '80s. There are colourful recollections of filming at Askrigg and a chat with Christopher Timothy, who played the part of James Herriot.

*'This lavishly illustrated book about James Herriot is one with a difference. As well as an account of the life of the world's most famous vet, Bill Mitchell gives a description of life in the northern moors and dales that the real James Herriot found so interesting.' Jim Wight*

## BEATRIX POTTER – Her Lakeland Years
### W. R. Mitchell

The compelling story of the real Beatrix Potter, based on interviews with those who knew her. Spread over the 40 years, these interviews recall memories stretching back to the time when Beatrix bought the now famous Hill Top farm at Sawrey in the heart of Lakeland. She was already internationally acclaimed for her series of 'Peter Rabbit' books and her local status was increased when she married William Heelis, a Hawkshead solicitor. The books gave her the means to purchase over 4,000 acres of land, which on her death in 1943 was bequeathed to the National Trust as her personal legacy to the Lake District.

The many archive and present-day photographs in this fully illustrated book place a new light on the Lakeland years of Beatrix Potter.

## WAINWRIGHT – His life from Milltown to Mountain

Bill Mitchell was a great friend of the legendary walker and writer, Alfred Wainwright. In this ground-breaking, richly anecdotal and personal book about Wainwright, he recalls Wainwright's young days in the Lancashire milltown of Blackburn and his fascination – as a lone walker – for wild places in Lancashire, along the Pennines and in the north-west extremities of Scotland.
*Fully illustrated. Hardback.*

*"I worked with AW on and off for five years but was still given a fresh glimpse of the great man in this smashing new book"*
*Eric Robson  Chairman, Wainwright Society*

*Visit www.greatnorthernbooks.co.uk*